Christian de Chergé
Spiritual Writings

MODERN SPIRITUAL MASTERS SERIES

CHRISTIAN DE CHERGÉ
Spiritual Writings

Selected, edited, and translated by
CHRISTIAN KROKUS AND HABIB ZANZANA

Maryknoll, New York 10545

Founded in 1970, Orbis Books endeavors to publish works that enlighten the mind, nourish the spirit, and challenge the conscience. The publishing arm of the Maryknoll Fathers and Brothers, Orbis seeks to explore the global dimensions of the Christian faith and mission, to invite dialogue with diverse cultures and religious traditions, and to serve the cause of reconciliation and peace. The books published reflect the views of their authors and do not represent the official position of the Maryknoll Society. To learn more about Maryknoll and Orbis Books, please visit our website at www.orbisbooks.com.

English translation and introduction copyright © 2025 by Christian Krokus and Habib Zanzana

Published by Orbis Books, Box 302, Maryknoll, NY 10545-0302

Translation of texts originally published in: *Dieu pour toujours: Chapitres de Père Christian de Chergé à la communauté de Tibhirine (1986–1996)*. Les Cahiers de Tibhirine Vol. 1. Montjoyer, France: Éditions de Bellefontaine, 2006.

L'Autre que nous attendons: Homélies de Père Christian de Chergé (1970-1996). Les Cahiers de Tibhirine Vol. 2. Montjoyer, France: Éditions de Bellefontaine, 2006.

© Les Éditions du Cerf/Bellefontaine, 2006

This project has been approved by the Association des écrits des 7 de l'Atlas.

All rights reserved.

No part of this publication may be reproduced or transmitted in any form or by any means, electronic or mechanical, including photocopying, recording, or any information storage or retrieval system, without prior permission in writing from the publisher.

Queries regarding rights and permissions should be addressed to: Orbis Books, P.O. Box 302, Maryknoll, NY 10545-0302.

Manufactured in the United States of America

Library of Congress Cataloging-in-Publication Data

Names: Chergé, Christian de, 1937-1996 author. | Krokus, Christian S., editor, translator. | Zanzana, Habib, editor, translator.
Title: Christian de Chergé : spiritual writings / selected, edited, and translated by Christian Krokus and Habib Zanzana.
Description: Maryknoll, NY : Orbis Books, [2025] | Series: Modern spiritual masters | Includes bibliographical references. | Summary: "Selected writings by Trappist martyr Christian de Cherge"—Provided by publisher.
Identifiers: LCCN 2024037225 (print) | LCCN 2024037226 (ebook) | ISBN 9781626986091 (trade paperback) | ISBN 9798888660645 (epub)
Subjects: LCSH: Chergé, Christian de, 1937-1996—Translations into English. | Christian martyrs—France. | Christian saints—France. | Cistercians. | Catholic Church and spiritualism. | Catholic Church—Relations—Islam. | Islam—Relations—Catholic Church.
Classification: LCC BX4700.C38 C34 2024 (print) | LCC BX4700.C38 (ebook) | DDC 230/.2—dc23/eng/20241123
LC record available at https://lccn.loc.gov/2024037225
LC ebook record available at https://lccn.loc.gov/2024037226

Contents

Acknowledgments	ix
Preface by Habib Zanzana	xi
Introduction by Christian Krokus	xv
FINAL TESTAMENT OF CHRISTIAN DE CHERGÉ, OCSO	1
CHAPTER TALKS	5
The Least of These Who Are My BROTHERS (Matthew 25:40) (Monday, January 27, 1986)	6
The Men of Fraternity (Wednesday, February 5, 1986)	8
"The Believers Are but BROTHERS, So Make PEACE between Your BROTHERS" (Q 49:10). (Friday, February 7, 1986)	9
The Sacrament of the BROTHER (Monday, February 10, 1986, Memorial of Saint Scholastica)	11
Foucauld: Islam along the Way (Friday, October 31, 1986)	14
From the "Muslim Brother" to the UNIVERSAL BROTHER (Friday, November 7, 1986)	15
Our Community as Such *hic et nunc* (Saturday, February 4, 1995)	18

vi | Contents

Our Community "in Its Environment" (Thursday, February 9, 1995)	20
"Those Who Pray among Others Who Pray . . ." (Thursday, February 23, 1995)	21
Untitled (Tuesday, April 4, 1995)	23
Who Is GOD Today? (Thursday, April 6, 1995)	24
"The Order Needs Monks More Than Martyrs . . ." (Tuesday, November 7, 1995)	27
Cistercian Heritage (Tuesday, December 12, 1995)	28
A "CONSTANCY" of Love [*amour*] (Thursday, December 14, 1995)	30
Christmas . . . and Us (Thursday January 4, 1996)	31
The Communitarian Character of the INCARNATION (Tuesday, January 30, 1996—after the Regular Visit from January 11 to January 20)	33
CST 86: "They JOYFULLY Make Their Way . . ." (Thursday, February 1, 1996)	34
And DEATH, Is It a Question? (Tuesday, February 13, 1996)	36
And the Other Congregations Represented Here? (Saturday, February 17, 1996)	37
Untitled (Thursday, March 14, 1996)	39
Of Good ZEAL . . . RB 72 (Saturday, March 16, 1996)	39
Letters	41
Tibhirine, September 26, 1979	42
Tibhirine, February 21, 1981	44

Tibhirine, June 12, 1982	45
Tibhirine, February 25, 1985	47
Tibhirine, June 26, 1985	49
Tibhirine, September 22, 1989	52
Tibhirine, November 30, 1992	54
Tibhirine, Beginning of 1994	55
Fez [Morocco], November 28, 1995	57
Retreat	58
The Mystery of the Visitation	59
The Well	61
Homilies	63
Untitled, December 6, 1970—Second Sunday of Advent, Year C	64
Trinity, June 17, 1984—Holy Trinity Sunday, Year A	67
CONVERSION and Cross, Christ, April 17, 1987—Good Friday, Year A	71
Called to Humility, March 24, 1989—Good Friday, Year C	73
The "Martyrdom" of Love [*charité*], March 31, 1994—Holy Thursday, Year B	76
The "Martyrdom" of Innocence, April 1, 1994—Good Friday, Year B	82
The "Martyrdom" of Hope, April 2–3, 1994—Easter Vigil, Year B	86

The Martyrdom of the Holy Spirit, May 22, 1994
—Pentecost, Year B   92

Untitled, April 13, 1995—Holy Thursday, Year C
(Fez, Morocco)   97

"You Are the Other Whom We Await,"
December 10, 1995—Second Sunday of Advent,
Year A   100

ARTICLES   105

Praying in the Church: Listening to Islam (1982)   106

The Mystical Ladder of Dialogue (1989)   115

Intermonastic Dialogue and Islam (1995)   158

Acknowledgments

CHRISTIAN KROKUS: My thanks to the members of the Association des écrits des 7 de l'Atlas for their trust and permission to translate Christian de Chergé's published texts, Bruno de Chergé for frequent and generous assistance and for the use of the cover photo, Jean-Jacques Pérennès, OP, for making the necessary introductions, Stephanie Saldaña for encouragement to pursue the project in the first place, Fr. Isaac Keeley, OCSO, and Fr. Emmanuel Morinelli, OCSO, at Spencer Abbey (Massachusetts) for informative conversations, the University of Scranton for granting a sabbatical during the 2023–24 academic year, the Lonergan Institute at Boston College for awarding a research fellowship also during the 2023–24 academic year, Robert Ellsberg for shepherding the manuscript to completion, Melinda Krokus for patience and support during long months apart, and Habib Zanzana for saying yes and making the work joyful.

HABIB ZANZANA: I would like to express my deepest gratitude to those who have been instrumental in the completion of this book. First and foremost, I extend my heartfelt thanks to Christian Krokus. Your thoughtful translations, profound contributions, extensive research, and collaborative spirit have significantly enhanced the quality of this manuscript. Your dedication and passion have brought immense joy and inspiration to this project. A special acknowledgment goes to my dear friend Steve Whitman. Your unwavering support, constant encouragement, and considerate feedback have been indispensable to me throughout this journey. I deeply value and cherish your friendship.

* * *

The ornament that appears on the chapter opening pages is "Bismillah ar-Rahman ar-Rahim," which in Arabic means "In the name of God, the Merciful, the Compassionate." It is the opening phrase of all but one chapter of the Qur'an and every Muslim prayer. Like the sign of the cross for Christians, the bismillah may mark the beginning of any significant undertaking for Muslims. The Islamic divine name of Mercy was very important to Christian de Chergé, who wrote a treatise comparing the Qur'anic notion of mercy with Pope John Paul II's encyclical *Dives in Misericordia*.

Preface

Habib Zanzana

The translation of spiritual writings by Christian de Chergé has been both a scholarly endeavor and a labor of love. As a professor of world languages and cultures, I was drawn to Christian de Chergé for the depth of his spiritual inquiries and his commitment to Islamic–Christian dialogue. This new translation of his writings aims to bring de Chergé's insights to a larger audience and to offer fresh perspectives on faith, love, obedience, the power of peace and fraternity, and the sharing of his vision for strengthening the relationships between Muslims and Christians.

The fact that I was born and raised in Dar El Beïda, a suburb of Algiers, in a Muslim family, surely nourished my desire to read, understand, research, and translate the spiritual works of Christian de Chergé. As a child during French colonization, I spoke Arabic at home and learned French in school. My teachers were dedicated French citizens, but we did not associate them with the colonial power. School was considered "sacred ground" in the sense that it was a privileged space, free of division and sectarianism, where Muslim children could learn, grow, and establish a solid foundation for a more promising future within an atmosphere of mutual respect and understanding.

My own interest in interfaith dialogue grew out of a beautiful friendship I built with Didier Daubechies, a

Belgian Franciscan living and working as a professor of architecture in Algiers. He had arrived in Algeria in 1968 and played a crucial role in fostering relationships with the Muslim community. Didier was exemplary in his commitment to the church, his students, and the wider Algerian population, particularly during the earthquake of El Asnam in 1980, which registered a magnitude of 7.1 and was considered the largest in the Atlas range.

I was finishing high school and preparing for the *baccalauréat* exam when I met Didier, who introduced me to the notion that God is love. Together we talked, meditated, enjoyed meals, and contemplated the mysteries of the divine. I would write him letters to chart my journey as a young Muslim seeking God in all things, fascinated by the idea of a shared interfaith vision. He would often remind me to be patient in prayer and to remain confident and steady in my faith and in my quest to understand the divine mysteries. Didier was a man of the church, older, wise, a spiritual mentor, and a guide who delighted in my youthful enthusiasm for religious spirituality. Ours was a brotherhood born out of admiration and respect for our respective Christian and Muslim traditions, and nurtured by regular meetings and conversations about faith, prayer, peace, family, education, charity, the sacred, and God's love toward humanity.

Perhaps that is why de Chergé's writings, particularly his friendship, conversations, prayers, and spiritual exchanges with Mohamed (Benmechay) have resonated so profoundly with me. They have motivated me to read his works in the original French and to make them available in English for readers of all faiths, thereby participating in what Christian Salenson describes as de Chergé's "theology of religious encounter" in his engagement with Islam.

Christian de Chergé was intellectually and spiritually

curious; he became especially fond of the Arabic language and was deeply moved by the beauty of Qur'anic verses. He found great joy in interspersing his homilies, chapter talks, and articles with Arabic expressions and quotes from hadiths of the Prophet Muhammad. He even called upon a Muslim to explain that "it is the secret of God's love, *sirr al mahabba*, that unites us." Dialogue for de Chergé was a spiritual practice rooted in genuine respect and appreciation for the other. His writings often explore the intersections of Christian and Muslim spirituality, revealing the common ground that can serve as a pathway for shared understanding, peace, self-giving love, and forgiveness.

Despite the escalating violence in Algeria during the 1990s and the direct threats they received from the GIA (Armed Islamic Group), de Chergé and his community of monks, after long and difficult discussions filled with uncertainty and anxiety, but also hope, chose discernment and decided to stay. He explains that "in doing so, we join our bishop's wish for the church to remain in this country and to share in the trials of the people who are linked to us either by birth, adoption, or in certain cases, by the grace of Baptism. This desire is not suicidal, even if it exposes us more to the dangers of the hour, which certainly carry [the risk of] a brutal death. No doubt we will have to come back to the fact that the gift of death is included in the gift of life." This generous and heartfelt commitment would ultimately cost them their lives.

De Chergé loved Algeria and the Algerians and sought to partake in the sufferings of others. His unwavering trust and confidence in God's presence and purpose are, no doubt, a testament to the enduring power of faith and the possibility of hope and redemption. He was also optimistic, wishing and praying that the civil war would soon end, and he remained energized and determined to stay in Algeria, caring for his church and participating fully in the rebuilding of the nation in times of peace. He conveys that same hopeful vision in a charming postcard he sent his friend Maurice Borrmans from Fez, Morocco, on November 28, 1995, in which he writes, "The boy and the girl [on the front of the postcard], in the same boat, on the sand, perhaps represent the image of tomorrow's Algeria, with a smile regained, and Peace imagined as a new distribution in a pluralistic society. . . . Of course, insecurity remains but this childlike hope must be given time to grow."

Through his writings and reflections on interfaith dialogue, fostering unity, martyrdom, the constancy of love, the call to humility, and the firm belief that "all seekers of God are brothers, that the quest is by nature eternal . . . and even that all men are brothers by virtue of their call from the Creator who fashioned them for the same purpose," de Chergé presents an enlightened and compelling vision of a world and a society on the path of spiritual development. We hope that this collection of Christian de Chergé's spiritual writings will serve as a bridge, connecting readers to his wisdom and inspiring us to carry forward his vision of a world united in peace, dialogue, mutual respect, and interreligious understanding.

Introduction

Christian Krokus

I am to talk to you about the "Cistercian contemplative" identity, an expression which, to be blunt, I don't much like. The phrase implies that contemplation yields something stable, an identity. But to my way of thinking, contemplation is either a form of continual searching or it is nothing at all. Here on this earth, it is a journey, a tension, a permanent exodus, the invitation to Abraham, "Come follow me."

That is how Blessed Christian de Chergé, OCSO (1937–1996), then the little-known prior of the tiny and poor monastery of Notre Dame de l'Atlas in Tibhirine, Algeria, opened his 1993 address to the leaders of the world's Trappist monasteries—monks and nuns—who were gathered at Poyo, Spain, for their general chapter.[1] Later in the talk, de Chergé recounts

---

1. "Trappist" is shorthand for members of the Order of Cistercians of the Strict Observance. The Cistercian Order, founded in 1098 at the Abbey of Cîteaux in France, is a renewal group within the Benedictine monastic tradition. The Trappists, founded in 1664 at the Abbey of La Trappe, constitute a reform movement within the Cistercian Order. Readers are likely familiar with the American Trappist monk Thomas (Louis) Merton (1915–1968), who belonged to the Abbey of Gethsemane in Kentucky.

the surprise of many European visitors to his monastery in Algeria, where the civil war of the 1990s had begun to ravage the country: "'How can you live in a house so insecure?' they always ask. But how can one really be a contemplative in a house that is too secure and well provided?"[2]

In those few words, we already discover several themes that will emerge more clearly across the pages of this collection. Christian de Chergé was a contemplative, and for him that meant rendering oneself available to the divine call to leave behind the comfort and security not only of one's native land, family, and language but also one's fixed ideas about God, the church, the religious other, and oneself. He was an adventurer who was engaged in a continual search, a permanent exodus, as he puts it, thrilled to discover the Gospel being witnessed in unexpected places, people, conversations, traditions, and gestures. He was courageous, accepting an invitation to live into vulnerability, to lower defenses, to disarm hearts, as he preferred to say, and inviting others to do so. He was convinced that the community could become permeable to the Holy Spirit, who wishes to lead all of us into unity and freedom through love. Joyful and positive, he was also self-assured, even stubborn, sometimes irritating confreres and superiors. Some mistook him for being naïve or idealistic, when in fact he was radically convinced of the truth of the Gospel. He embraced the goodness of creation, including all human beings. He lived in loving and awe-filled wonder, and he refused to succumb to cynicism, resentment, and rivalry.

The contemplative tension to which de Chergé refers in the quotation above lies between an ever-strengthening personal attachment to Christ and, because of that attachment,

---

2. John Kiser, *The Monks of Tibhirine: Faith, Love, and Terror in Algeria* (New York: HarperCollins, 2002), 132–33.

Introduction | xvii

an ever-expanding horizon of encounter with God beyond the visible limits of the church. That dynamic is most evident in his exuberance for dialogue with Muslims and his explorations of Islam. He was convinced that already, in God, a Christian–Muslim communion of saints exists that is being embodied here and now in Christian–Muslim friendships, prayer, learning, hospitality, and mutual self-donation. Readers are most likely to know about Christian de Chergé in relation to the events leading up to and surrounding the kidnapping and death that he suffered along with his six companions, and they will find, especially in his later writings, de Chergé reflecting at length on the relevant circumstances and questions. However, long before those dramatic last days, he was making significant contributions to our understanding of authentic Christian spirituality—in many respects anticipating the categories and language of Pope Francis: encounter, fraternity, going out—especially as it relates to encounter with Muslims and Islam, and that is where we have focused much of this collection.

BIOGRAPHY

Christian de Chergé was born on January 18, 1937, in the city of Colmar, in the Alsace region (Haut-Rhin) of France. He descends from a long line of aristocratic military leaders, and the family motto, *Recte semper*—*Always upright*, anticipated the integrity and directness that Christian would exhibit as a leader in the military and at the monastery. When de Chergé was a young boy, his father, who was then a colonel in the French army, was stationed in Algeria, at the time a French colony, during World War II. In those years (1942–1945), Christian had his first encounter with Muslims. Curious one day about a group of Muslim men praying in public, Christian inquired with his mother, whom he considered his "first church." She taught her little boy that they were praying to God, albeit in a different manner than was familiar to their Catholic family, and the lesson took root.[3] At the conclusion of the war the family returned to France, settling near Parc Monceau in the eighth arrondissement of Paris, where Christian attended Catholic schools. By the age of eight he had already expressed a desire to become a priest, and in 1956, upon completion of secondary school, he entered the archdiocesan seminary of Carmes, which is attached to the Institut catholique de Paris.

In 1958, still a seminarian, de Chergé was called up for military service during the Algerian War of independence. Having joined a new unit of the French army called the Specialized Administrative Sections (SAS), in 1959 he returned to Algeria for the first time since his youth. He was stationed near Tiaret in the northwest part of the country and, as the title of the unit implies, his duties were largely administrative, coordinating and supporting the activities of the local civil, educational, and health services as well as Algerian and French law enforcement. The SAS was essentially a French effort to win or keep the "hearts and minds" of the local Algerian Muslim populations. It was during those years that de Chergé befriended Mohamed, whose identity Fadila Semaï has confirmed as being Cheikh Benmechay (1912–1959),[4] and about whom

---

3. Marie-Christine Ray, *Christian de Chergé: Prieur de Tibhirine* (Montrouge, France: Bayard Éditions, 1998), 20–21.

4. Fadila Semaï, *L'ami parti devant* (Paris: Éditions Albin Michel, 2016). Semaï explains that "Mohamed" was a generic name used by French residents and soldiers to refer to any Algerian man. Christian de Chergé refers to his friend in writing only as "Mohamed." Had he, like many other French soldiers, uncritically adopted the belittling practice of erasing Algerians' given names? Or, as would be fitting, was he protecting his friend's identity and that of his friend's family by not

Christian Salenson has said de Chergé "would live the rest of his life in the horizon of his meeting."[5] The forty-seven-year-old Algerian Muslim policeman and father of eleven worked closely with the twenty-two-year-old French Catholic SAS officer and even took him under his wing.[6] During the rounds they made together, the two engaged in long conversations about God, Algeria, family, and other matters, and Christian even visited the home of Mohamed Benmechay for occasional couscous dinners.[7] Their friendship, however, which transcended national and religious lines, proved to be too much, too controversial for some of the locals, who hatched a plot to do harm to Christian while he accompanied Mohamed to a relative's home. Having recognized upon arrival the danger his young charge was in, Mohamed inserted his own body between those of the would-be attackers and their intended target, managing to extract Christian and himself from the immediate threat. However, a few days later, the same men hatched a second plot, this time luring Mohamed to a construction site where they murdered him for having protected a French officer.[8] It is an episode and a friendship to which Christian de Chergé returns again and again in prayer and writing. It was the proximate catalyst for his discovery of a vocation that would involve returning to Algeria as a Christian praying alongside Muslims.

---

using his given name? Semaï reports that de Chergé tried unsuccessfully to meet with members of Benmechay's family in later years.

5. Christian Salenson, *Christian de Chergé: A Theology of Hope*, trans. Nada Conic (Collegeville, MN: Liturgical Press, 2012), 27.

6. Christian de Chergé describes Benmechay as having ten children; Semaï reports eleven.

7. The use of "Mohamed Benmechay" in this instance aims to honor the man's given name. However, to maintain continuity with de Chergé's usage, hereafter we use "Mohamed."

8. Semaï, *L'ami*, 137–39.

De Chergé credited his conversations with Mohamed as having "liberated" his own faith and having convinced him of the beauty and authenticity of the Islam lived among working-class Algerians with little formal education.[9] After his Algerian friend saved his life, and knowing that this same friend was now endangered, Christian promised to pray for him. Mohamed teasingly responded: "I know that you will pray for me, but you see, Christians do not know how to pray."[10] De Chergé took the comment to heart, and it served as part of his motivation for joining the Trappists at Notre Dame de l'Atlas, where he would belong to Christians who knew how to pray and who prayed in a way that was visible and recognizable to their Muslim neighbors. Mohamed's sacrifice not only inhabited Christian's thinking and deciding, but it also inhabited his prayer. He tells us that "every Eucharist makes him intimately present to me in the reality of the Body of Glory where the gift of his life took on its full dimension 'for me and for the many.'"[11] Mohamed had laid down his life for his friend, making it clear to de Chergé that Muslim witnesses, in and through their embodiment and practice of Islam, could be participants in the redemptive work of the Son and the Holy Spirit.

After spending eighteen months in Algeria, de Chergé returned to Paris to complete his seminary education. He was ordained a priest in 1964, and his first assignment was as a chaplain at the Basilica of Sacré Coeur de Montmartre, where in addition to saying masses and hearing the confessions of pilgrims, he was responsible for youth formation and for accompanying parishioners on trips to the Holy Land. From the earliest days of the assignment, however, de

---

9. Ray, *Christian de Chergé*, 47.
10. Salenson, *Christian de Chergé*, 24.
11. Salenson, 26.

Chergé had already discerned a call to monastic life. In 1969, having promised his bishop at least five years of service to the Archdiocese of Paris, he applied to and entered Notre Dame d'Aiguebelle, a Trappist monastery in the Rhône-Alps region of France. From the beginning he was forthright with his new abbot about his desire, upon completing the novitiate, to transfer to the monastery of Notre Dame de l'Atlas in Tibhirine, Algeria, next to the town of Médéa, about 70 km south of Algiers, where the monks would adopt the informal motto, "Those who pray among others who pray."

In 1971 de Chergé arrived at Tibhirine, where he was given the job of guest master in the early years of his formation. That position put him in direct contact with his Muslim neighbors and opened the door to a regular experience of what he called "existential dialogue," or what Catholics would later call the "dialogue of life."[12] From 1972 to 1974, he was sent to Rome for a formal education in Islamic studies at the Pontifical Institute for the Study of Arabic and Islam (PISAI), where he studied under and developed a lifelong friendship with Maurice Borrmans, M.Afr. (1925–2017), who also served as director of academics. For his thesis, de Chergé explored the religious history of Algeria, including figures as diverse as the Roman Catholic theologian and bishop St. Augustine (354–430), and the Algerian Muslim spiritual writer and nationalist-warrior Emir 'Abd al-Qâdir (1808–1883).

Life at the monastery was not without its challenges in his early days there. As the most ardent supporter of dialogue with Muslims and the only one trained in the study

---

12. Pontifical Council for Interreligious Dialogue, *Dialogue and Proclamation* §42, https://www.vatican.va/roman_curia/pontifical_councils/interelg/documents/rc_pc_interelg_doc_19051991_dialogue-and-proclamatio_en.html.

of Islam, de Chergé's enthusiasm could rub some of the other monks the wrong way. He was known, for example, to remove his sandals when entering the chapel the way Muslims remove their shoes when entering a mosque, to fast in the Islamic way during the month of Ramadan, to greet guests in the traditional Muslim way of placing his hand on his heart, and, with the permission of his superior, to deliver weekly lessons on Islam to the other monks during their chapter meetings, an experience some referred to as "proselytizing."[13] In 1976, as part of his final profession of vows, de Chergé shared a text with his brothers titled "The Meaning of a Call," in which he reflected on the convergences and points of mutual illumination between his own fledgling monastic vocation and Islamic spirituality. The tensions became serious enough that de Chergé questioned his place at Notre Dame de l'Atlas, even flirting with the idea of joining a newly formed religious community known as the Monastic Fraternities of Jerusalem.

In 1979, after a two-month retreat in Assekrem at the Saharan hermitage of Charles de Foucauld (1858–1916)—himself a former Trappist, from the Alsace region, and a profound influence upon de Chergé—Christian recommitted to his vocation at Tibhirine. While he became more sensitive to his relationships with the other monks, he remained just as enthusiastic and certain about his particular calling to Catholic–Muslim encounter. In that same year, Claude Rault, M.Afr. (b. 1940, eventual bishop of Laghouat), instituted a series of meetings for Catholics in Algeria who were engaged in dialogue with Muslims and learning about Islam. The group met at Notre Dame de l'Atlas twice a year for three days per gathering, and de Chergé became Rault's principal co-organizer. In 1980, some members of the local

---

13. Kiser, *Monks of Tibhirine*, 53.

Alawiyya Sufi-Muslim confraternity approached de Chergé about joining the nascent meetings, and from that point forward it became an interreligious space and a spiritual oasis for de Chergé.[14] The group took the name *Ribât as-Salaam*, the Bond of Peace, from the expression in Paul's Letter to the Ephesians (4:3).

For many years the members of Tibhirine were governed by a rotating cast of superiors assigned to them from their founding monastery, Notre Dame d'Aiguebelle. However, in 1984, Notre Dame de l'Atlas was granted the status of simple priory, which came with the right to choose, internally, the community's leadership, although in other respects the priory remained dependent on the founding monastery. By that point, de Chergé had gained enough trust of enough of his brothers that they elected him as their prior, a position he would hold until the end of his life. He set to work developing closer relations with each of the men, and he made it a priority to stabilize the situation at the monastery, which had seen a number of younger candidates come and go over the years. At the general chapter held in 1984 at Holyoke, Massachusetts, Dom Christian, the world's newest Trappist leader, successfully lobbied his confreres to send several volunteers from the larger European monasteries to join his community in Algeria. The challenges he and his brothers faced, however, were about to increase exponentially.

The 1990s are often referred to as the black years (*années noires*) or the black decade (*décennie noire*) in Algeria. In those years, the country was consumed by a civil war that according to some estimates claimed almost two hundred

---

14. Sufism, sometimes referred to as the mystical tradition of Islam, is roughly analogous in its structures to Catholic religious orders. The Alawiyya confraternity (*tariqa*) is named for its founder, the Algerian Sheikh Ahmad al-Alawi (1869–1934).

thousand lives, the vast majority of which were Algerian Muslim civilians. Indeed it has been described as a dirty war (*sale guerre*) because of the rampant targeting of civilians and extreme acts of violence on both sides. The Armed Islamic Group (GIA) was the main Islamist militia fighting against the army, which in 1992 had seized control of the government, disbanded the Islamic Salvation Front (FIS), which was Algeria's main religious political party, and canceled the national elections, which the FIS was poised to win. The GIA had already targeted Algerian Muslim political and religious leaders as well as academics and journalists, when on October 31, 1993, they decreed that all foreigners must leave Algeria within thirty days or risk becoming "responsible for their own sudden deaths."[15] Within a week of the November 30, 1993, deadline, the GIA followed through on their threat, seriously wounding an Italian man and killing men from Spain, France, and England as well as a Russian woman. On December 14, 1993, twelve Croatian petroleum engineers and technicians, who were frequent visitors to the monastery, were murdered, and on December 24, 1993, Sayah Attiyah (d. 1994), the leader (*emir*) of a local GIA branch and the man personally responsible for orchestrating the massacre of the Croatians, arrived at the monastery gate as the monks were preparing to celebrate the Christmas Vigil mass.

The Christmas Eve scene will be familiar to anyone who has seen Xavier Beauvois's 2010 film *Of Gods and Men* (*Des hommes et des dieux*).[16] It is not the event that leads to the monks' abduction, but it was their first brush with mortal danger. When the emir and his men first meet Christian, it

---

15. Kiser, *Monks of Tibhirine*, 138.
16. Xavier Beauvois, dir., *Des hommes et des dieux* (Culver City, CA: Sony Pictures, 2010).

is inside the monastery gate. Christian insists either that the men leave their weapons outside the monastery proper or that they speak outside the gate. When they step outside, the emir demands money, medicine, and Frère Luc, who was the oldest member of the community. He was also the monastery physician, and he ran a free medical clinic for the village, sometimes seeing over a hundred patients in a day and always willing to treat anyone who sought care, no questions asked, "even the devil," as Christian liked to quote him. When Christian denies all three demands, the emir frustratedly informs the monastic prior that he has no choice, a thinly veiled threat. Christian then pauses, collects himself, and responds: "Yes, I do have a choice."[17] Rather than provoke a violent reaction, Christian's conviction seems to have opened a moment of authentic human connection. As a result, the emir withdrew his demands for the moment, and when Christian informed him that the monks were about to celebrate the birth of Jesus, the Prince of Peace, the emir apologized and said he did not know. Several commentators have suspected that, after that encounter, the emir extended his personal pledge of protection over the monastery. And apparently, some of the men in the emir's entourage, knowing the privileged status of Jews and Christians in the Qur'an, remarked that they would distinguish the monks as "Christians" from other "foreigners" living in Algeria.

 The monks were understandably shaken by the encounter, and in the aftermath a majority expressed a desire to leave Algeria. However, as de Chergé led them through a series of discussions and votes—a process of discernment—other senses emerged. First, the monks agreed that whatever choice they made they would make as a community. They would leave together, or they would stay together.

---

17. Ray, *Christian de Chergé*, 181.

Then, despite the protests of the local civil authority (*wali*), who strongly encouraged them to leave—but offered military protection if they stayed—and despite the hesitation of the abbot general of the Trappists, Dom Bernardo Olivera (b. 1943), the monks eventually discerned a decision to remain unarmed in the country. Just the same, they left open the possibility of departure, should their presence become either unwelcomed by or a danger to their Algerian Muslim neighbors.

Throughout the conflict, the monks maintained their commitment to nonviolence as well as their position of neutrality, referring to the Algerian army as the "brothers of the plain" and the rebels as the "brothers of the mountain." However, as de Chergé insists, neutrality could never mean the monks would, like Pilate, feign to wash their hands of all responsibility for the conflict or its consequences. Rather, it must mean that the monks, as guests of Algeria, would remain free to love everyone involved in what they considered a fratricidal war, a freedom de Chergé believed would be irreversibly compromised were they to choose, or appear to choose, a side. In this regard Christian de Chergé departs from the example of his spiritual mentor, Charles de Foucauld, who in another political context made different choices. We might say that de Chergé sought to realize, even more radically, the "universal fraternity" to which Foucauld famously aspired.

As de Chergé reflected during the aftermath of the events of December 24, 1993, he realized that, although Sayah Attiyah was responsible for so much bloodshed and terror, he could not ask God to kill him. He could, however, ask God to disarm him. And yet, he wondered, how could he ask that Sayah Attiyah be disarmed unless he, Christian, and his fellow monks were also disarmed, not from physical weapons of course, but from their own biases about the

Introduction | xxvii

humanity or lack thereof of the rebels, about Muslims and Islam, and even about the meaning and value of safety? Going forward, de Chergé adopted as a regular prayer: "Disarm me; disarm them."[18] Finally, in de Chergé's insistence, "I have a choice," we glimpse his embrace of the theological virtue of hope, always leaving room for conversion. He was not interested in a spiritual or theological perspective that could not foresee or account for the free response of the centurion (Mt 27:54), the good thief (Lk 23:32), or even Judas (Mt 27:3). We might include the emir and his men, the Algerian soldiers, and ourselves.

In subsequent years the situation in Algeria only became more dire. From 1994 to 1996, thousands of Algerian Muslim citizens lost their lives, and eleven European members of various Catholic religious orders were assassinated, most of them close friends of the monks of Tibhirine. Among Christian de Chergé's responsibilities as prior of the community was the delivery of chapter talks to his brothers, typically about some aspect of the *Rule* of St. Benedict or the OCSO *Constitutions*. He usually offered three per week, unless he was traveling, focusing on a particular theme for several weeks at a time. The themes included, to name a few, fraternal love, patience, humility, and the writings of St. Bernard of Clairvaux (1090–1153). As the violence escalated, he devoted his talks and homilies to developing the ecclesial and theological grounds for remaining in the country without armed protection, embracing what Stephanie Saldaña has called a "theology of staying put."[19] The last two themes he covered in his chapter talks were "the situation of the church *hic et nunc*"

---

18. Salenson, *Christian de Chergé*, 31.
19. Stephanie Saldaña, "An Impossible Hope: Three Men in Syria Showed Me What Jesus Looks Like," *Plough* 13 (Summer 2017): 44–52, 51.

and "the charism of martyrdom." During Holy Week and into the Easter season of 1994, he gave a series of homilies under the titles "The Martyrdom of Love," "The Martyrdom of Innocence," "The Martyrdom of Hope," and the "Martyrdom of the Holy Spirit," across which he recovers the meaning of martyrdom as a vulnerable witness to love, hope, and faith that builds up the other, including one's enemy, rather than as a glorious death that depends on the diminution of one's rival. When the abbot general told him that the order had "more need of monks than of martyrs," de Chergé responded that "there is no contradiction," if martyrdom is understood as a daily giving away of oneself to one's brothers and neighbors in ordinary acts of love.[20] After all, if one's life has already been given away in love, then it cannot be taken. Not surprisingly, a favorite biblical verse of de Chergé's was John 10:18, "No one takes [my life] from me, but I lay it down on my own."

In the early hours of March 27, 1996, Christian de Chergé and six of his fellow monks were kidnapped, and on May 21, 1996, they were killed, although some questions about the circumstances of their deaths remain unanswered. While this is a collection of Christian's spiritual writings, he never spoke or wrote alone. As he says of himself and his fellow monks at the opening of his article "The Mystical Ladder of Dialogue," theirs is "a communal witness" and "nothing can be understood apart from the common presence and fidelity of all of us to our humble daily reality, from the garden gate to the kitchen, to *lectio divina*." Paul (Luc) Dochier (1914–1996), Paul Favre-Miville (1939–1996), Michel Fleury (1944–1996), Christophe Lebreton (1950–1996), Christian (Bruno) Lemarchand (1930–1996), and Célestin Ringeard

---

20. Bernardo Olivera, *How Far to Follow? The Martyrs of Atlas* (Kalamazoo, MI: Cistercian Publications, 1997), 12.

(1933–1996) were also kidnapped and killed. Jean (Amédée) Noto (1920–2008) and Jean-Pierre Schumacher (1924–2021) survived the crisis and eventually relocated to the monastery's annex in Fez, Morocco (today in Midelt, Morocco). On December 8, 2018, Pope Francis beatified the Tibhirine seven along with twelve other Catholic martyrs of the Algerian civil war.

THREE CONTEXTS: MONASTICISM, ISLAM, POSTCOLONIAL ALGERIA

Readers who are unfamiliar with de Chergé's wider body of writing may find it helpful to keep in mind that he was a monk, that his monastic vocation was thoroughly integrated with his encounter with Islam and dialogue with Muslims, and that he was acutely aware of France's legacy of colonialist exploitation and violence, including his and his monastery's part in that legacy.

Christian de Chergé was a close reader of the documents of the Second Vatican Council and papal encyclicals as well as the writings of various modern theologians and philosophers, from Charles Peguy (1873–1914) and Teilhard de Chardin (1881–1955) to Emmanuel Levinas (1906–1995) and Etty Hillesum (1914–1943). He also read modern Muslim intellectuals such as Mohamed Talbi (1921–2017) and the modern Catholics who engaged with Islam such as Louis Massignon (1883–1962) and Youakim Moubarac (1924–1995). He also wrote extensively—well over a thousand pages have already been published—including several studies either delivered as talks or published in various journals. The preponderance of his writing, however, was undertaken in a monastic context: homilies, chapter talks, reports, letters of spiritual direction, and so on. It is astonishing to think that most of what he wrote and the profound spiritual wisdom he shared were initially intended for an audience of a dozen or so intimate companions, depending on which monks or guests were present at the monastery on a particular day. It is equally impressive, given how considerable were his pastoral and administrative responsibilities—not to mention that Cistercian monks spend seven liturgical "hours" plus mass in prayer every day—that he found time to write anything at all.

Nearly all of Christian de Chergé's spiritual-theological thinking and writing was the fruit of the monastic practice of *lectio divina*, sacred reading, the slow, patient, contemplative reading by which one listens for a word from God with the "ear of the heart," as St. Benedict said. Traditionally one applies *lectio divina* to the Bible, or perhaps to the *Rule* or a Christian classic, but de Chergé applied it to everything, not only to the Bible but also to the Qur'an, not only to texts but also to conversations and historical events, and even to whole religious traditions. In his writing, therefore, de Chergé is primarily concerned to identify encounters with the divine and invite readers into them, rather than, for example, to work out the finer theological points that may be implied in such encounters with the Word.

Christian de Chergé has been called a "a man of unity."[21] His vocation as a Christian and a monk was profoundly integrated with his love of Islam and his commitment to Muslim friends. We have already seen how Catholic–Muslim encounters marked major moments of his religious journey, and readers will observe how frequently he refers to Islamic sources, whether Qur'anic verses, hadith (sayings of the Prophet Muhammad), conversations with Muslim neighbors, Muslim writers, and so on, even when writing about topics that appear to be exclusively Christian, such as

---

21. Ray, *Christian de Chergé*, 133.

the Trinity or the Cross. He was always building bridges, or to use his favorite image for dialogue, the mystical ladder, always standing on the rungs that connect the two uprights of Christianity and Islam. So, for example, in a homily for the Feast of the Cross (September 14, 1993), de Chergé narrates a conversation he had with a Sufi-Muslim friend:

> "And what about the cross?" I was asked recently by one of our Sufi friends. "What if we were to talk about the cross?" "Which one?" I asked him. "The cross of Jesus obviously." "Yes, but which one? When you see an image of Jesus on the cross, how many crosses do you see?" "Perhaps three. Two for sure. There is the one in front and the one behind." "And which is the one that comes from God?" "The one in front," he said. "And which is the one that comes from men?" "The one behind." "And which is the more ancient?" "The one in front. It's like this: men could not have invented the other except that God had already created the first." "And what is the meaning of this cross in front, of this man with his arms outstretched?" "When I stretch out my arms," he said, "it is in order to embrace, to love." "And the other?" "It is the instrument of love that is distorted and disfigured, of hatred fixing in death the gesture of life."
>
> The Sufi friend had said: "Perhaps three?" This third cross, wasn't it I, wasn't it he, making the effort which drew both of us to separate ourselves from the cross "behind," the cross of evil and sin, in order to cling to the one "in front," the cross of victorious love?[22]

---

22. Salenson, *Christian de Chergé*, 81–82.

xxxii | Introduction

The Catholics gathered for mass that day, living in Algeria and regularly interacting with Muslims, were surely aware of the Islamic denial of the crucifixion of Jesus. De Chergé demonstrates that even if Muslims deny the fact of Jesus's death, potentially they already understand and embrace something of what the cross means to Christians. In fact, he will say in his article "Intermonastic Dialogue and Islam" that Christians and Muslims are engaged in a shared "adventure of meaning." At the same time, he shows Catholics that it is possible to come to a deeper understanding of their own beliefs and tradition through the eyes and the witness of their Muslim neighbors and friends. Notice that for de Chergé the exchange itself was an instance of embracing the "more ancient" cross, the one created by God. The very act of coming together, learning, and seeking points of convergence is to participate in Christ's open-armed embrace, and to leave behind the fear, shame, and insecurity that cause us to deny the voice and the dignity of others. We also see in that homily that de Chergé worked to render Christian beliefs more accessible to his Muslim interlocutors. Along those lines, he commissioned a cross for the chapel of Notre Dame de l'Atlas with a resurrected Christ, where the crown of thorns is absent and the nails in Jesus's hands and feet are replaced by points of light, precisely because it would be more inviting to Muslim sensibilities. One thinks also of the spontaneous common prayer he shared with a Muslim visitor to the monastery despite ecclesial hesitations around such things. It was an experience he described as having "incarnated his hope."[23] If the Catholics in the chapel for that Feast of the Cross in 1993, or readers of the following pages, find themselves feeling uneasy about Christian de Chergé's assumptions of unity and refusal to see even the

---
23. Ray, *Christian de Chergé*, 112.

most fundamental theological disputes as grounds for separating Christians and Muslims, perhaps that is his point. When his friend Maurice Borrmans cautioned Christian against moving too quickly on some aspect of Christian–Muslim dialogue and admonished him to "listen to your brothers," de Chergé responded: "Which ones?"

Finally, if readers are at all familiar with de Chergé's writing, they probably know his *Testament*, and for good reason as it is quickly becoming a classic of Catholic spirituality. He began writing the *Testament* on December 1, 1993, which marked the expiration of the deadline the GIA had given for foreigners to leave the country. It was also the anniversary of the death of Charles de Foucauld, and de Chergé instructed his family to open the *Testament* in the event that he too should suffer a violent death. We have included a translation here, which we placed at the beginning of the collection. In addition to its powerful themes of love, forgiveness, peace, and Christian–Muslim communion, we must not lose sight of another important element, namely, de Chergé's commitment to Algeria. He tells us that his life was "GIVEN to God and to this country" and that for him "Algeria and Islam are . . . a body and a soul." He loved the country and its people, its cultures, languages, and history, its Islam and its church, and he hoped and planned to survive the civil war in order to be part of the country's rebuilding process. If he and his monastic brothers refused to take sides during the war, it was because they had adopted Algeria as their home and all Algerian people as their family. In 1978 de Chergé applied for Algerian citizenship as an expression of his vow of stability, but his application was never acknowledged.[24] Disappointed, he was nevertheless reminded that he and his fellow Europeans were guests of the country.

---

24. Kiser, *Monks of Tibhirine*, 49.

Several lines into the *Testament*, de Chergé asks of his community, church, and family:

> May they associate my death with so many equally violent other ones, forgotten through indifference or anonymity. My life has no more value than any other. Nor any less. In any case, it does not have the innocence of childhood. I have lived long enough to know that I am complicit in the evil that seems, alas, to prevail in the world, and even in that which would strike me down blindly.

Needless to say, that is not just pious talk. He is acknowledging his role in the French colonial legacy of violent exploitation in Algeria, and he attempts to redirect his readers' attention away from the few French Catholic victims of the civil war and toward the many Algerian Muslim victims who suffer in part because of that colonial legacy.[25] It is a question as to whether an institution that has been responsible for a social problem can also be part of its solution, but it is possible to see much of Christian de Chergé's preaching and writing, as well as the dialogues in which he participated and the decisions he made with his brothers, as imperfect but deliberate attempts at unwinding the legacy of exploitation and violence he and his brothers inherited and to some degree perpetuated. With that context in mind, one begins to notice how often de Chergé gives voice to ordinary Algerians and how prominently the wishes of his neighbors factor into his own commitment to stay in Algeria, when the easier thing would have been to retreat to the safety of France.

---

25. Christian Salenson, "Christian de Chergé: Un chrétien face à la violence," *Islamochristiana* 43 (2017): 195–215, 200.

TEXT SELECTION, ORGANIZATION, AND STYLE

The English-language literature on Christian de Chergé and the monks of Tibhirine is growing, and readers who desire a deeper dive might begin with (just to mention books): John Kiser's *The Monks of Tibhirine*, Christian Salenson's (translated) *Christian de Chergé: A Theology of Hope*, Bernardo Olivera's *How Far to Follow?*, Jane Foulcher's *Reclaiming Humility*, and Christophe Lebreton's (translated) journal, *Born from the Gaze of God*.[26] Christian Salenson refers to the witness of Notre Dame de l'Atlas as a "sign for our time offered to all by the Spirit."[27] The same could be said of the entire Algerian church of that era. To learn more about the extraordinary witness of Léon-Étienne Cardinal Duval (1903–1996) and Henri Teissier (1929–2020), the successive archbishops of Algiers who exercised a profound influence upon Christian de Chergé, and especially about Pierre Claverie, OP (1938–1996), the bishop of Oran and last Catholic martyr of the Algerian civil war, who was killed with his Muslim friend and driver Mohamed Bouchikhi (1975–1996) on August 1, 1996, readers may begin with Jean-Jacques Pérennès's (translated) *A Life Poured Out*.[28]

For this project, we translated only texts that were already published in French. Excerpts of some of the writings we include here have been translated elsewhere as parts

---

26. Jane Foulcher, *Reclaiming Humility: Four Studies in the Monastic Tradition* (Collegeville, MN: Liturgical Press, 2015), 243–306; Christophe Lebreton, *Born from the Gaze of God: The Tibhirine Journal of a Martyr Monk (1993–1996)*, trans. Mette Louise Nygard and Edith Scholl, OCSO (Collegeville, MN: Liturgical Press, 2014).

27. Salenson, *Christian de Chergé*, 22.

28. Jean-Jacques Pérennès, *A Life Poured Out: Pierre Claverie of Algeria*, trans. Phyllis Jestice and Matthew Sherry (Maryknoll, NY: Orbis Books, 2007).

of secondary works, but the one text in our collection that was translated previously in its entirety is the *Testament*. In addition to chapter talks, homilies, academic articles, and his *Testament*, we included the text of a retreat and several letters to Maurice Borrmans. Christian de Chergé kept up a voluminous correspondence with family, friends, Cistercian superiors, Vatican officials, members of other monasteries, candidates for Notre Dame de l'Atlas, government representatives, Muslim and Christian thinkers, editors of journals, and so on. However, thus far the only portion of his correspondence to be published as a stand-alone collection is the volume of letters that his friend Maurice selected and shared.

One reason we opted more for homilies and chapter talks than for academic studies is that they directly reflect the monastic context in which de Chergé was living and writing. In addition, they are shorter and thus lend themselves to more meditative attention, perhaps even to *lectio divina*. Not to worry, however, as many of the themes he addresses in longer articles, he also touches upon in the shorter, more personal writings. We have arranged the texts by genre and within each genre by chronology. Those who decide to read straight through a particular genre will surely notice the rising tension, but also the mounting resolve, hope, love, and creativity in Christian's words as the monks' situation becomes more precarious. We selected generously from the last period of de Chergé's writing, not least because therein he has made a significant and lasting contribution to the Catholic understanding of martyrdom.

A few stylistic choices merit mentioning. First, whether in manuscript or when typing, Christian de Chergé very frequently capitalizes entire words and phrases for emphasis. On the other hand, his capitalization of pronouns that refer either to Jesus or God is inconsistent. We have preserved de Chergé's usage in every case. He also very often employs ellipses. Sometimes he does so for dramatic effect, inviting the hearer or reader to pause and reflect on what has just been said or written. Other times, the ellipses may reflect moments where he pauses to collect his own thoughts before continuing. We have preserved the bulk of his ellipses, but we have occasionally eliminated them when they inhibit his flow of thought. The use of parentheses is always de Chergé's. The use of square brackets is always ours. If de Chergé's text included a footnote, we raised the reference to the body of the text and placed it in brackets. We also made some of de Chergé's many implicit Bible references explicit by including a citation in brackets. At times de Chergé plays against each other two words that have distinct but close meanings in French, but which normally would be translated by just one word in English. To handle these cases we typically use slightly different English words, and in many instances we include the French term in brackets so that readers may follow de Chergé's line of thought. Examples include *Verbe/parole*, translated here as *Word/word*, *espérance/espoir*, translated here as *hope/hopefulness*, and *charité/amour*, usually translated here simply as *love* but occasionally as *charity/love*. De Chergé regularly employs masculine terms such as "man," "men," "mankind," "fraternal," "brother," "he" and "himself," even when referring to universal categories. When fitting, we occasionally opted for gender-neutral terms such as "humanity," "people," "human beings," and "one." However, the usage of masculine terms is so pervasive that we left most of them in place, trusting readers to recognize, not uncritically, that de Chergé was communicating in a different era, in a male-dominated monastic-ecclesial context, and through a masculine-inflected language.

Where they exist, we used official or authoritative English translations of texts that de Chergé quotes in French. The main examples include passages from the Bible, for which we employed *The Catholic Study Bible*, and from the Qur'an, for which we used *The Study Qur'an*.[29] For official statements of the Catholic Church we relied on the archives at https://www.vatican.va/. For official documents of the Order of Cistercians of the Strict Observance we drew from the archives at https://ocso.org/. Occasionally, de Chergé's phrasing of a quoted text is idiosyncratic, whether because of the French translation he used or because he was quoting from memory. If his phrasing is central to a point he makes, we translated his version directly. Finally, we hope readers will find their engagement with Christian de Chergé as rewarding as we have found it to be.

---

29. *The Catholic Study Bible*, ed. Donald Senior et al. (Oxford: Oxford University Press, 1990); *The Study Qur'an*, ed. Seyyed Hossein Nasr et al. (New York: HarperCollins, 2015).

Final Testament of Christian de Chergé, OCSO

During Algeria's civil war of the 1990s, the Armed Islamic Group (GIA) announced a November 30, 1993, deadline for all foreigners to evacuate the country or risk being assassinated. In that context of heightened risk, on December 1, 1993, Christian de Chergé began writing this Testament, *which has become a modern classic of Catholic spirituality. December 1 is also the anniversary of the violent death of Charles de Foucauld (1858–1916), a profound spiritual influence upon de Chergé. Christian sent the* Testament *to his youngest brother, Gérard, with instructions not to open it until his death. The monks were kidnapped in the early hours of March 27, 1996, and killed on May 21, 1996; and Christian's* Testament *was opened on the feast of Pentecost, May 26, 1996.*

Notes: In everyday parlance adieu *means "goodbye." However, we translated de Chergé's* A-Dieu, *hyphenated in the manuscript, literally as "To-God" to capture the hope he expresses that he and his "friend of the last moment" may meet again in God. We translated* s'envisage *in the opening line/title as "foreseen" to cap-*

From Bruno Chenu, ed., *Sept vies pour Dieu et l'Algérie* (Montrouge, France: Bayard Éditions, 1996).

ture Christian's premonition in relation to the unfolding events. However, at the root of s'envisage *is the sense of "face," which connects the title to de Chergé's reference to God's face appearing in the face of his "friend of the last moment." De Chergé was influenced by the philosopher Emmanuel Levinas (1906–1995), especially regarding the notions of the Face and the Other. Finally,* Amin *is the Arabic version of* Amen, *and* insh'allah *means* God willing *in Arabic.*

When a "TO-GOD" is foreseen . . .

If it should happen one day—and it could be today—that I become a victim of the terrorism which now seems intent on engulfing all foreigners living in Algeria, I would like my community, my Church, and my family to remember that my life was GIVEN to God and to this country. May they accept that the one Master of all life was not a stranger to this brutal departure. May they pray for me: For how could I be found worthy of such an offering?

May they associate my death with so many equally violent other ones, forgotten through indifference or anonymity. My life has no more value than any other. Nor any less. In any case, it does not have the innocence of childhood. I have lived long enough to know that I am complicit in the evil, alas, that seems to prevail in the world, and even in that which would blindly strike me down. I would like, when the time comes, to have a moment of clarity that allows me to beg forgiveness of God and of my brothers in humanity, while at the same time forgiving wholeheartedly the one who will have gotten to me.

I could not wish for such a death; it seems important to me to state this. I do not see, in fact, how I could rejoice if the people I love were indiscriminately accused of my murder. It would be too high a price to pay for what will perhaps be called the "grace of martyrdom" to owe it to an Algerian, whoever he may be, especially if he says he is acting in fidelity to what he believes to be Islam. I know the contempt that can be heaped upon the Algerians as a whole. I also know the caricatures of Islam that a certain Islamism inspires. It is too easy to soothe one's conscience by identifying this religious path with the fundamentalism of its extremists. Algeria and Islam, for me, are something else; they are a body and a soul. I have proclaimed this often enough, I believe, in view of what I have received [from Islam], finding there so often that true strand of the Gospel learned at my mother's knee, my very first Church, precisely in Algeria and, already, with respect for Muslim believers.

My death, surely, will appear to confirm those who hastily called me naïve or idealistic: "Let him tell us now what he thinks!" But those people should know that my most burning curiosity will finally be liberated. I will be able, please God, to immerse my gaze in that of the Father, to contemplate with him his children of Islam as he sees them, completely illuminated by the glory of Christ, the fruit of his Passion, permeated by the gift of the Spirit whose secret joy will always be to establish communion and restore the likeness, while playing with the differences.

For this life lost, totally mine and totally theirs, I give thanks to God, who seems to have willed it entirely for JOY, in and despite everything. In this THANK YOU, which expresses everything in my life from now on, I of course include you, friends of yesterday and today, and you, O friends of this place, alongside my mother and my father, my sisters and my brothers and their families: the hundredfold granted as was promised!

And you too, my friend of the last moment, who will

not have known what you were doing. Yes, for you too I offer this THANK YOU, and this "TO-GOD," whose face appears in yours. May it be granted that we meet again, happy thieves in paradise, if it pleases God, the Father of us both. AMEN! AMIN! Insh'allah!

Algiers, December 1, 1993
Tibhirine, January 1, 1994

Christian

Chapter Talks

"Chapter" is a polyvalent term in the Western monastic tradition. It can mean the section of the Rule of St. Benedict that the monks are reading or about which the abbot is teaching. It can mean the meeting at which such reading or teaching is taking place. It can name the room in which the meeting is occurring. It can also refer to the gathered community itself. When he was elected prior of Notre Dame de l'Atlas in 1984, Christian de Chergé inherited the responsibility of teaching his brothers through the medium of chapter talks. He typically delivered three per week, with exceptions made for travel, hosting visitors from the Order's leadership, or other interruptions to the schedule. He wrote them out by hand, and as far as we know he read them verbatim, because the talk had to fit into the same period during which the monks prayed the office of Terce before returning to work. De Chergé pursues the same theme across a few weeks, exploring it from various angles, and often one talk flows more or less uninterruptedly into the next. The titles of the talks are de Chergé's. According to the editors of the published collection in French, we do not have de Chergé's chapter talks from his first year as prior. They pick up in spring 1985.

From Christian de Chergé, *Dieu pour tout jour: Chapitres de Père Christian de Chergé à la communauté de Tibhirine (1985–1996)* (Montjoyer, France: Éditions de Bellefontaine, 2006).

In the following four talks de Chergé emphasizes that in both Christianity and Islam, while there are scriptural and theological grounds for applying the category of fraternal love universally, ultimately it is the responsibility of the believers to determine how widely they understand others to be "brothers." He also introduces the notion that human relationships, including Christian–Muslim friendships, are potentially quasi sacramental, visible signs of a divinely ordered reality. Note: A hadith is typically a saying of the Prophet Muhammad.

The Least of These Who Are My BROTHERS (Matthew 25:40) (Monday, January 27, 1986)

"The Word became BROTHER!" To be able to translate the message of the Incarnation we must rediscover the theme of the BROTHER at the heart of the Gospel and the teachings of Jesus.

Sometimes Jesus stages a scene with two brothers, as in the parable of the two sons—the prodigal and his older brother—or the two [brothers] of whom one says "yes" and the other "no" [Mt 21:28–32]. It happens that Jesus is taken to task by two brothers over questions of inheritance (Lk 12:13), but he does not allow himself to be diverted from his way by resolving such conflicts. It happens that Jesus is surrounded by brothers, James, John, Simon, and Andrew, or he has a bond of friendship with an entire family, as at Bethany. It also happens that Jesus is sought by his mother and his brothers (see the three Synoptics, Lk 8:21 and parallels) and his response is sharp: "Whoever does the will of my Father, that one is my brother, my sister, my mother" (Mt 12:50) or even "those who listen to the word of God and practice it." In saying so, Jesus is describing the very attitude of the Son, who came to do the will of the Father. To imitate the Son in His relation to God is to be prepared to leave behind parents, brothers, sisters, etc. Luke (14:26) goes even further when he has Jesus say: "If anyone comes to me and does not hate his father, mother, brothers, sisters, and even his own self, he cannot be my disciple."

The brother, like the parents, serves as a natural reference to express what should be an attachment to the Lord, the love of Him who presents himself as eternally more linked to men and to the Father than any natural bonds. Those bonds are relative, provisional, threatened by disputes, ingratitude, and ultimately death. Those bonds can be denied, which is the great threat posed to them by the likely persecution of the disciples. Jesus weeps for the death of a brother; though he takes in the suffering of the two sisters, he does not present himself as the brother of Lazarus, for the latter is and remains his FRIEND. In fact, according to the Gospel, while he was alive, Jesus called no one "my brother" or "brother" as is so typical among those who are close. He will call his apostles "friends" or even "my children."

And then, in the surprise of the Easter announcement entrusted to Mary Magdalene, according to Saint John: "Go find my brothers and tell them that I am ascending to my Father and your Father . . ." (Jn 20:17; some omit the possessive: *my brothers*). The parallel text from Matthew speaks of the risen Jesus's encounter with the two Marys: "Go, announce to my brothers to go to Galilee, and there they will see me" (28:10). Here too the mention of "brothers" appears so unusual that certain manuscripts transcribe it as "disciples." However, in Matthew (25:40) we find the revealing text: "Whatever you did for one of these least brothers of mine, you did for me." Here there is unanimity among the manuscripts. . . . But the discussion has not yet closed: Are his BROTHERS solely the disciples chosen from among the little ones of the world? Or are they all men, as long as they do not swell with pride but count themselves among those in need of God?

The Men of Fraternity
(Wednesday, February 5, 1986)

Is Christ the bearer of a universal message of fraternity? The answer to the question posed as such is clear. But is the person who does not accept this message in faith my brother? The least we can say is that the Church has long hesitated to answer "yes." One may wish to be a "universal brother," like Brother Charles [de Foucauld], in the name of Christ . . . while regretting not being able to extend the title of brother to anyone who does not confess the name of Christ. Perhaps this is a point on which the doctrine has evolved over the ages, reaching the quasi certitude recorded by Vatican II and summarized by the simple affirmation of Paul VI: "Every man is my BROTHER."

A recent history of the Christian people is titled *The People of Fraternity*. It's undeniable that Christianity's message of LOVE has brought those who have accepted it to live a new fraternity whose pole and model is CHRIST, in whom every man can recognize himself. But we must go further, grounding this entirely novel (and original) fraternity theoretically and spiritually. It's no longer just a matter of the flesh-and-blood relationships within the vast family of the sons of Adam. It's not even about the bond of FAITH, for while faith creates a very real and specific fraternity among Christians, it is not enough to guarantee the eternity of this fraternity. "Faith will pass away," the sacraments will pass away. . . . Love will not pass away; the fraternity established in the paschal love of Christ, "the firstborn of many brothers" (Rom 8:29), will not pass away. It is a fact of the Gospel that Jesus speaks of HIS brothers only after the Resurrection. In this Easter context, the Incarnation finds its completion: not only God in our flesh, but our flesh in God; not only God becoming our brother, but this brother, who is fully one of us, totally in God.

Just as we do not in fact know what the body of glory is, so we do not know what the fraternity of the beyond is, the fraternity that AWAITS us, already given entirely in Christ as a relationship open to infinity and offered to ALL. The proper mode of the Father's relationship to men is paternity, from which all paternity in heaven and on earth takes its name (Eph 3:15). The proper mode of the Son's relationship to men is fraternity . . . but there is a difference. Paternity is co-eternal with the Father, but fraternity is not co-eternal with the Son. Of itself, oneness can have no equal. Thus fraternity expresses the KENOSIS by which the Son entered into multiplicity, not ashamed to call us brothers in time and for eternity (reread Heb 2:10–18 and the accompanying notes in the Ecumenical Translation of the Bible). The content of this qualification as BROTHER is none other than his FILIAL attitude infinitely multiplied in the same Spirit.

"The Believers Are but BROTHERS, So Make PEACE between Your BROTHERS" (Q 49:10). (Friday, February 7, 1986)

This verse, already cited at the beginning of our religious approach to the notion of BROTHER, may seem welcome at the start of a year consecrated to Peace; it would appear to support the initiative in favor of PEACE that John Paul II undertook by inviting to Assisi all the religious leaders for a common approach to prayer and a fraternal sharing of their respective spiritual values. However, this verse received the same strict interpretation already discussed in relation to the Gospel: the BELIEVERS, for most commentators and for the vast majority of the faithful, are the MUSLIMS. Other verses will confirm the thesis: Only the followers of Islam are truly brothers in God. We should study the tradition, the hadith.

One hadith begins like Saint Paul in many of his counsels to the Church: "Do not be jealous of one another . . . do not hate each other, do not turn your backs on each other . . . be servants of God and BROTHERS; Muslims are BROTHERS to each other; they are neither unjust, nor unreliable, nor liars, nor contemptuous of each other. . . . The Muslim, in his entirety, is sacred for his Muslim BROTHER, whether it concerns his life, his fortune, or his honor." By all means, let's ask our mystical friends, who will tell us that all seekers of God are brothers, that the quest is by nature fraternal . . . and even that all men are brothers by virtue of their call from the Creator who fashioned them for the same purpose. Many will say that as a minimum the BELIEVERS include the "People of the Book" and that there is fraternity in Abraham.

A well-known hadith states: "Unless you desire for your BROTHER what you desire for yourself, your faith is incomplete." The commentary I consulted adds: "It would be good to hear this from all brothers, whether unbelievers or Muslims, but true love desires that the non-Muslim becomes Muslim, since that is what we ourselves are and desire to remain, and for the Muslim brother to persevere in Islam, for that is the deepest desire of the believer."

Generally speaking, if we say that DESIRE makes the brother (rather than the realization of desire), then all men are as much brothers of the Muslim as they are of the Christian, since both desire that their faith be shared without themselves having fully achieved the realization of that desire. They may [both] carry [the desire] all their lives . . . and thus achieve together the meaning of a fraternity that is not fulfilled here below but in God, master and object of their common desire.

"Yes, those who fear God are in the midst of the Garden and the springs: 'Enter here in peace and security.' We have removed whatever rancor was in their hearts. They are BROTHERS on beds of repose facing each other" (Q 15:47).

The Sacrament of the BROTHER (Monday, February 10, 1986, Memorial of Saint Scholastica)

It's a happy coincidence that allows us to finish this series of reflections on the BROTHER by honoring, through Saint Scholastica, an exemplary fraternal relationship both on a human and a spiritual level. If we trust Saint Gregory, we have two fraternal destinies, those of Benedict and his sister, twins from birth, closely associated in their quest for the Unique One, drawn into an intimate colloquy on the joys of heaven, becoming for each other the sign and quasi sacrament of the communion of saints, and united in death a month apart as though in a last ecstasy.

We've spoken about the sacrament of the BROTHER. What does it mean? A sacrament is a visible and imperfect human sign of an invisible and perfect divine-human reality. The BROTHER in question, invisible and perfect, is the CHRIST of Easter, whose companion in a glorified humanity like his own is his mother MARY. The Incarnation, as we have said, introduced into God this fraternal relationship, our only gateway to the Trinitarian mystery in which we now have our place, *filii in Filio . . . fratres in Unum*. . . . That's the meaning of Christ's fraternal prayer in Jn 17:23: "May they be ONE as we are ONE, I in THEM (fraternal mystery) as YOU are in ME (Trinitarian mystery of paternity and filiation)." The CHURCH is the sacrament, the visible sign, of the communion of son and mother, of their two fraternal natures in God. In that sense Christians are called to show mutual consideration and love, creating model, exemplary relationships without hesitation on either side in the name of Christ, who calls on them to signify it together. Fraternal love is an essential trait of the Face of Christ that requires at least two to signify truly and properly: "See how they love one another" [Tertullian, *Apologeticus* 39].

More broadly, we can say that wherever the Spirit is free to act in the heart of a man, he fashions a brother of this Christ of glory, and, as a Christian, I must not fail to recognize these family traits. And if I don't see them, I must believe in them in the name of Him who loved even unto death. My faith in Christ is expressed through faith in the person called to become one of these least ones who are the brothers of Jesus. As a Christian, every person must become for me, even unknowingly, a sacrament of Christ the brother, an object of the same fraternal love of Christ who receives us both from his Father and sees us together as his brothers in the light of our ultimate and perfect identity. And this is why love for man and love for God are not two loves but one. "No one can claim to love God whom he does not see, if he does not love his brother whom he does see" (1 Jn 4:20), that is, if he does not love this visible brother as a sacrament of the invisible BROTHER. "He who does not love his brother is not of God" (1 Jn 3:10).

From fall 1986 into spring 1987, de Chergé offered a series of talks on the theme of religious conversion, including a long treatment of the case of St. Augustine (354–430) and a shorter treatment of St. Thérèse of Lisieux (1873–1897). He also devoted nine talks to the conversion of Charles de Foucauld (1858–1916), from which we present two.

Foucauld, like de Chergé, was from an aristocratic family with a celebrated military pedigree. After a period of self-indulgence and agnosticism, while on a secret exploration of Morocco, Foucauld experienced a religious awakening that eventually led him back to his native Catholic faith. In 1890, he entered the Trappist monastery of Notre Dame des Neiges in France, but later he transferred to a simpler, poorer monastery in Syria. He then left the Trappists altogether and spent several years serving the Poor Clare nuns in Nazareth as a way of imitating the hidden life of Jesus, that is, the years Jesus spent growing, learning, and working among family and neighbors. In 1901, he was ordained a priest and moved to Algeria, first as a kind of military chaplain and later as a hermit-missionary, living among the Touareg Muslim population in Tamanrasset, where he sought to become a "universal brother." With the outbreak of World War I Foucauld constructed a fort for his own protection and that of his neighbors. French soldiers also stored weapons in the fort, and on December 1, 1916, Foucauld was killed there by some raiders, perhaps German aligned.

During his own vocational crisis of 1979, Christian de Chergé spent two months in retreat at Foucauld's hermitage at the remote Assekrem, about eighty kilometers from Tamanrasset. De Chergé was deeply influenced by the witness of Foucauld, and the parallels between the two men's lives are apparent. After recounting the main points of his biography, Christian pays special attention in his talks to Foucauld's initial attraction to but eventual rejection of Islam, which, after his conversion to Catholicism, Foucauld considered a false religion, insufficiently committed to love and filled with errors (although he remained open to meeting Muslims as a brother). In conversation with Foucauld's example, de Chergé was clearly examining his own vocation as a monk in Algeria in dialogue with Muslims.

Notes: Brother Albéric is the name that was assigned to Charles de Foucauld when he entered the Trappists. Laylat al-Qadr, *the Night of Power-Destiny, falls near the end of the Islamic month of fasting, Ramadan. It also marks the initial revelation of the Qur'an to the Prophet Muhammad.*

Foucauld: Islam along the Way
(Friday, October 31, 1986)

Foucauld would say that he imagined a long intellectual journey ... and the result, as we know, is striking: it left him forever defeated, CONQUERED, intellectually defenseless but fulfilled. To be able to move forward, he never ceases to examine the times and revisit the past. The publication he completes, that of the report of "his reconnaissance" in Morocco for the Geographical Society, allows him to identify clearly an essential influence upon his return to God, that of ISLAM. There are, on this point, some writings of his that are clear, notably letters to Castries and [François-Henry] Laperrine. The latter will even write to General [Émile] Nieger upon his return from Morocco that Foucauld had wanted to become Muslim.

In a letter to Henry de Castries of 1901, Brother Albéric himself recognizes: "Islam is extremely seductive; it has seduced me inordinately ... ," and then, "it pleases me very much because of its simplicity, simplicity of dogma, simplicity of hierarchy, simplicity of morals." Some biographers of the interwar period have more or less consciously glossed over the importance of the encounter with Islam as a decisive moment on his path to conversion "as if the Holy Spirit could not lead someone to ABBA through this encounter" ([Jean-François] Six). In 1883, therefore, Foucauld pursued with tenacity and realized his indomitable dream of being the first European to enter the "land of refusal to submit,"

BLED es SIBA, Morocco. Accordingly, he accepted the financial constraints of his judicial counsel, the dangers of the route, and the humility of disguising himself as a Jewish merchant. But this truly spiritual experience involved some strictly human ends, "for his pleasure." He enters into an excess that will be discovered later and that he had already largely manifested in his private life.

There is also the expression of a SOLITARY instinct that made him prefer the isolated adventure to the collective combat (a moment so exhilarating), as later he preferred the eremitism of the desert to the Cistercian cenobitism. He wanted to be the first, the most original, the most audacious, the only . . . he is still struck by an ISLAM that honors God as the Greater, the First. He writes, again to Castries: "ISLAM has produced in me a profound upheaval . . . the sight of this faith, of its souls living in the continual presence of God, has made me glimpse something GREATER and MORE TRUE than mundane occupations: *ad maiora nati sumus.*"

From the "Muslim Brother" to the UNIVERSAL BROTHER (Friday, November 7, 1986)

Foucauld was a complicated soul, attracted to extremes, capable of excess, of [enjoying] good food as well as denial, of luxury as well as poverty. If he was initially seduced by Islam, it was, as we saw, because of its contrasting SIMPLICITY. However, upon reflection, such an absolute and excessive temperament could not for very long remain enamored of a religion that presents itself as the path of MODERATION, the middle way accessible to all. He will have the same problem with Saint Benedict. He required the exceptional.

In 1901, fifteen years after his conversion, that becomes clearer to him as he denounces what he calls a radical vice at the very foundation of Islam: "Islam does not have enough contempt for creatures to be able to teach a love of God worthy of God: without chastity and poverty, love and adoration remain very imperfect; for when one loves passionately, one separates from anything that might distract, even for a minute, from the loved one, and one throws oneself and loses oneself totally in him" (letter to Henry de Castries, July 15, 1901). From 1883 to 1886, clearly things were less clear-cut.... He always acknowledged that Islam opened a breach into which he threw himself headlong. It gave him a sense of the GRANDEUR of God when he was mired in trivial matters.

[Islam] served as a launching pad for his conversion and his [Catholic] faith. The seduction was all the stronger because of his experience of the Sahara, of the desert, where man is in a continual state of ADORATION: "In that deep calm, amidst that magical nature, I reached my first shelter in the Sahara. One understands in the quiet of such a night, the belief of the Arabs [Muslims] in a mysterious night, *Laylat al-Qadr*, in which the sky opens, the angels descend to earth, seawater becomes fresh, and every inanimate thing in nature prostrates itself to ADORE its Creator." The influence continued, daily, during his journey through Morocco. François-Henry Laperrine writes: "This year of life in the midst of convinced [Muslim] believers strikes the last blow to Foucauld's skepticism. He admired the strength that the Moroccans drew from their faith, as much that of the fanatical and fatalist Muslims as of the Jews who remained unshakably attached to their religion despite centuries of persecution." Once returned to God, he felt called to CONFIRM his BROTHERS: "I want to accustom all the inhabitants, whether Christians, Muslims, Jews, or idolaters, to regard me as their brother, the universal Brother" (letter to his cousin [Marie de Bondy], 1901).

When Christian de Chergé gave the next five chapter talks—from a section titled "The Situation of the Church, hic et nunc,*"— the community had already experienced the Christmas Eve visit described in the Introduction. Violence in Algeria had escalated dramatically, and as de Chergé mentions in the first talk, several members of other Catholic religious orders had been assassinated. In the early weeks of 1995, the monks took a series of votes to determine whether and under what circumstances they would consider leaving Algeria. In the talk that immediately precedes this group (January 31, 1995—Our Community and Our Church), de Chergé reviews the results of those votes, which reveal (a) a unanimous desire to remain united as a monastic community whether at Tibhirine or elsewhere and (b) strong majority desires to remain at Tibhirine as long as possible and, if necessary, only to relocate to another Muslim-majority country, most likely Morocco but possibly Tunisia.*

Christian frames the votes and the monks' discussion of them as a process of discernment informed by the monastic vow of stability. He also emphasizes a recent call from the Algerian bishops for a kernel / core (noyau) *of Catholics to remain in the country despite the dangers. Finally, he describes three rings of communal discernment to which he believes the vow of stability commits the monks. The innermost and most intimate ring is the dialogue undertaken by the monks themselves. A second ring includes dialogue with and within the local church, especially with the present and former archbishops of Algiers, Henri Teissier and Léon-Étienne Cardinal Duval respectively, but also with the leadership of the Cistercian Order. A third ring includes dialogue with Algerian neighbors, almost all of whom are Muslim. The discernment also gives rise to examinations of the monks' roles as healers and witnesses, themes which de Chergé treated in his Holy Week, Easter Vigil, and Pentecost homilies of 1994, and an examination of the character of God and God's relationship to the suffering of the Algerians.*

Notes: A wali *is the chief local civil administrator, somewhere between a governor and a county commissioner in the American system. The "community" in "Our Community as Such" and "our little thing" in "Those Who Pray" both refer to the monastery of Notre Dame de l'Atlas. The Abbey of La Trappe, referred to in "Our Community as Such," was suppressed and confiscated in the wake of the French Revolution. When they returned, the monks had to rebuild the ruined property and severed relationships. A "regular visit," mentioned in "Those Who Pray," refers to the canonical responsibility of a parent monastery to inspect the conditions of the monasteries under its care. In "Who Is GOD Today?" we added the quotation marks around "the Jews" to indicate that de Chergé is referring directly to the language of the Gospel of John and not globally to the Jewish people.*

Our Community as Such *hic et nunc* (Saturday, February 4, 1995)

The majority of our community has expressed a desire of belonging to the permanent CORE [of Algerian Christians]. In doing so, we join our bishops' wish for the Church to remain in this country and to share in the trials of the people who are linked to us either by birth, adoption, or in certain cases, by the grace of Baptism. This desire is not suicidal, even if it exposes us more to the dangers of the hour, which certainly carry [the risk of] a brutal death. No doubt we will have to come back to the fact that the gift of death is included in the gift of life.

But if this is not "collective suicide," as the former *wali* called it, that is, first of all and concretely, because the risk does not seem inescapable to us. There is still room, in this confrontation with those who threaten us as foreigners and/or as Christians, for a conversion of hearts. Saying this, let's not forget the price that Jesus paid for the immediate conversion of the thief or the centurion, and, more remotely but also directly, for ours. In the case of Jesus, there was no suicide. Although he chose to give his life freely, he did not kill himself. Moreover, for us as for him, it was a step forward in OBEDIENCE that allowed him to accept this "cup" from the Father. No one, not even the Son, can claim [to live] the madness of love alone. It requires the assent of the Trinitarian communion. For us, for each one of us, the assent of the community is also necessary. And for the community as such there must also be an additional call from the Order and/or from the local Church. Hence the importance of the dialogue in which we have engaged with our bishop from the beginning.

Let us seriously consider what he said recently at the meeting of the presbyteral council: "What joy it would be for us, and what a promise for the future of our Church in Algerian society, if we could go through this crisis with our friends and then rebuild with them, in a partnership endowed with a new legitimacy. We might think, as a symbolic example, about the situation of LA TRAPPE in its environment, if the community of the monastery can survive the crisis." It must be said immediately that this partnership in the adventure would also derive its legitimacy from the free sacrifice of our eight brothers and sisters who have already paid with their lives for the fidelity that we are trying to express. We must remain sensitive to the sign that the Church instinctually seeks in community. Saint Bernard often said that a monastery is a small Church, an *ECCLESIOLA*. This sign of the Church, which can no longer be given [in this part of Algeria] either in formally constituted parishes or among diocesan priests devoid of faithful, who will give it if not communities like ours that are linked to the shared mission that remains the same today as yesterday: to give one's LIFE like Jesus did?

Our Community "in Its Environment" (Thursday, February 9, 1995)

We have privileged as much as possible the permanence of our community as such, at the center of this core of the Church, which finds itself called to signify the GIFT that Jesus made of his life in favor of all people, and in favor of the Algerians of today. And our joy, though a bit troubled and unsettled, is to feel that many of those who remain, like us, despite everything, lean on us, even if they do not tell us so. That is what our bishop meant to express to the presbyteral council. You will certainly have noticed that he spoke about the meaning of our presence, if it should survive this painful crisis, "in its ENVIRONMENT." The mention of our vicinity is appropriate. We cannot be the sign of a GIFT if no one is there to receive it or to desire it. Better said, we cannot claim to give them Jesus in any way without receiving JESUS from them in some way. That is the condition of the Incarnation. There is mutual interdependence. Many have not received Jesus. But those who have received him, he leads them to become what he himself was, not just Christians but, more than that, children of God.

I also note that in speaking about our immediate environment as constitutive of the sign we are, our bishop has more or less consciously reiterated what for us is an obvious fact: it would not be easy, perhaps even impossible, to believe that, presently, we could be this sign anywhere but here. Finding ourselves in any environment other than remaining in Algeria—under the pretext of greater safety or for any other reason—would seem arbitrary to me. Not only because I do not see where we could be "out of danger" in this country at the moment, but also because whatever consolation our preservation would bring to our little Church, so mistreated, it would be paid at the cost of a loss of meaning, insofar as the environment would no longer be as integral a part of our presence as it can be here. It would be a bit like keeping fish from a river in a jar.

Of course, we can imagine that this connective tissue could be woven with a new community one day at a time . . . but if the basic conditions of mutual trust and sharing of life are not met, there is the risk of the graft being rejected. It is true that if we have difficulty seeing how this could be, it is because, today, together, we are still of the mind that we are not there yet, and that it is precisely our environment which tells us so.

"Those Who Pray among Others Who Pray . . ." (Thursday, February 23, 1995)

We have all contributed over the years (thirty-three years . . .) to the demonstration that our "little thing" has remained VIABLE by the grace of God. The presence of the elders whom I just recalled allows us to speak of continuity . . . while those who arrived at Atlas after independence understand themselves in relation to the new political status of Algeria as well as the unique religious face that independence has somehow restored to this country. They could not come here without accepting in advance one and the other. We became, almost instinctively, the only community of the [Cistercian] Order immersed in a totally non-Christian landscape. Some said that this specificity really wasn't important, since the monastic vocation is the same everywhere. It was enough to know that the environment allowed us to live it, and most of our visitors over the years have agreed that this was the case for us on the condition that we maintained our boundaries. We even found ourselves in conditions of poverty, simplicity, and dependency, which are lacking elsewhere and which have brought us closer to the origins of Cîteaux. The Algerian law was for us a good "guardrail." The sirens of consumerism did not really reach us.

In 1982, a Visitor (Timadeuc) told us: "I feel very much at ease among you; one often says that at Atlas there is something very special, but that bothers me because I think that the monastic (Cistercian) vocation should and can be the same everywhere, because it's universal. You are 99 percent exactly like Timadeuc." I then answered that what interested me was precisely the 1 percent . . . where the difference seems to reside. It is there that we maintain our own personality, and where our calls from God are truly respected and taken into account, since in fact we are precisely here and not at Timadeuc (nor at Bellefontaine, nor Tamié, nor Aiguebelle).

We should be grateful to Dom Bernard Lefebvre for reminding us of this during his first regular Visit in 1983 by asking us to find our way to a certain autonomy: "Atlas is not Aiguebelle, and it is not right that your Abbot has for so long been from Aiguebelle. Your autonomy is not tied to your numbers, which are what they are, but to your specific situation as you have defined it for yourselves." Already in 1975 we wanted to be "Those WHO PRAY among others WHO PRAY." It required taking a careful measure of our "place" to arrive at that definition, which is both simple and precise: "those who pray among others who pray. . . ." The new threat weighing upon us changes nothing about this reality. We are most secure by remaining aware of it. It is the SIGN that God ventured in gathering us here.

Untitled
(Tuesday, April 4, 1995)

I had envisioned looking with you at our life from the triple perspective that Father [Pierre] Talec suggests in his book on rooting SERENITY in grace: he talks about GRATUITY, WISDOM, and FIDELITY. These mini-chapters since January have taken a different turn, more existentialist you could say. However, we find basically the same trilogy in the "characteristics" that Father Manuel discovered in our Church of Algeria. In his report to the major superiors, he spoke of GRATUITY, FRIENDSHIP, and FIDELITY. Maybe we should take up this thread again when I return. . . . In the meantime, it's good to keep it in mind since it's close to what we've been sharing with each other over these last months. For now, here are two or three little things I offer this morning for your reflection:

1. Our brother doctor [Luc] . . . Let's recognize that he treats everyone. He always has. Those are the ethics of his profession. A sick or wounded person causes the borders between camps to be erased, whatever their personal convictions. The doctor may even feel closest to whoever is most affected, most helpless, most threatened. That is the case with our Brother Luc. Certainly his caregiving involves all of us, in the name of our communal bond and vocation, and unites us to "this" doctor. In other words it is not only his business, even if in practical matters of care only he is capable of intervening. If we don't make ourselves available for offering other forms of aid that don't carry the same moral and humanitarian urgency

(like giving a cup of water to someone who is thirsty), it is still the case that each of us is called to deepen a dimension that remains ours, that of HEALING. All of Algeria is seriously ailing, and we can all contribute to the healing that should concern all its members. We are thus in the very perspective of Jesus, the shepherd who wished to be the "doctor" of souls. Prayer is, for us, a privileged place of this ministry. But in everyday life, in our relationships, we can bring this commitment of mercy and compassion, expressing our desire for healing (e.g., the confessor).

2. We made the decision to STAY . . . and to remain here. We do not see ourselves elsewhere today. Our choice was confirmed by the authorities of our Church, but also and above all by the calls from our environment. There is, in this decision, something like a renewal of the GIFT that we have made of our lives to the people, to these men and these women. This choice must remain free. That's the Gospel today coming through the threat we are facing.

Who Is GOD Today?
(Thursday, April 6, 1995)

In the difficult debate in chapter 8 of Saint John (the Gospel of these days), we see very clearly two approaches to God confronting each other, that of "the Jews" and that of Jesus. Two experiences too, although we have the feeling that only Jesus speaks from direct experience. "The Jews" [of John's Gospel] are tempted to contain God within their Law . . . and as a result, it becomes an idol, a word of death. This is why I want to return, before moving on and especially before Holy Week, to the question that was asked of us during the meeting of the major superiors: "what is the experience of God that we are called to live in the situation where we find ourselves?"

This is a question that can occupy each of us during these Holy Days. We should try not to respond too quickly, in the manner of a catechism. The eternal question is the one Jesus made so personal: "And you, *you*, who do you say that I AM?" [Mk 8:29]. At the meeting, we had to share, instantly, unexpectedly. Maybe it was a good thing. There's no escaping the question and its pertinence. At the same time, there's an obligation to receive other answers as *partial* as mine, and just as *vital*, both in progress. So I wanted to share with you, simply, what I said about it . . . perhaps to invite you to enter more deeply into reflection on our God.

Five observations about God:

1. a God who ACCOMPANIES . . . who undoubtedly precedes, but of whom we can say "He is there, He was there."
2. a God who hates DEATH but who has broken through and overcome the fear of death, who has integrated death into life.
3. a God who LOVES the Algerian people . . . and who has chosen to need us, me, to tell them so, to show them (a fairly low level of love shown to them in Europe, in France in particular, according to the latest polls).
4. a God who remains SILENT . . . more than he speaks. And I understand this silence better given the tendency to make him speak too much, to distort his Words [*Paroles*].
5. a God who has no contempt for any creature . . . who forbids me to judge, to condemn anyone. Greater than my heart.

Christian de Chergé presented his last chapter talks under the heading "The Charism of Martyrdom." Aware of the increasing probability that he and his fellow monks, like so many Algerian Muslim civilians and the members of other Catholic religious orders, may suffer a violent end, de Chergé uses these last talks both to encourage his brothers in their communal decision to remain and to offer ecclesial and theological grounds for understanding the meaning of the deaths they may be called to suffer. The category "martyrdom of love" is often associated with the witness of St. Maximilian Kolbe (1894–1941), but de Chergé recovers an older use of the term from the Salesian spiritual tradition, specifically the teachings of St. Jane de Chantal (1572–1641), founder with St. Francis de Sales (1567–1622) of the Visitation Order of nuns. In good Salesian fashion, St. Jane argues that the more valuable martyrdom is not a dramatic and glorious death, but the martyrdom that involves giving oneself to others freely in ordinary, everyday acts of love.

De Chergé imparts the same lesson to his brothers. He also corrects what he sees as too exclusive a focus on the cross in the Catholic understanding of redemption. He insists on the mutuality of redemption and Incarnation, even arguing that Incarnation, rather than the cross, is the primary key for interpreting the meaning of Jesus's death. His exploration of the OCSO Constitutions and the governing texts of other religious congregations for references to martyrdom, death, Incarnation, and redemption demonstrates his deeply communitarian-ecclesial disposition. The final talk in this section, "On Good Zeal," represents the last one we have from Christian de Chergé. He and his six companions would be kidnapped eleven days after he delivered it. The ellipsis at its conclusion is thus particularly poignant.

Notes: "Our Brothers in Bosnia," from "The Order Needs MONKS," refers to the Trappist Abbey of Mariastern in Banja Luka, whose monks remained in Bosnia during the Yugoslavian war of the 1990s. Tamesguida, Algeria, from "A 'CONSTANCY' of Love," is the town where the massacre of the Croatian engineers and technicians took place on December 14, 1993. Gilles Nicolas (1936–2011), referenced in "Christmas . . . and Us," was a parish priest in Médéa, Algeria, and a close friend and frequent visitor of the monks at Tibhirine. Staouëli, from "And the Other Congregations Represented Here," is a town outside Algiers where the original Trappist foundation in Algeria was established in 1843; it closed in 1904. In French the same word, Pâques, refers both to the Jewish celebration of Passover and the Christian celebration of Easter. Therefore, we usually translate Pâques as Pascha to avoid any Passover–Easter confusion while preserving the sense of movement, transformation, passing-over that is often integral to de Chergé's use of the term. Orthodox Christians frequently refer to Easter as Pascha. Finally, CST 86 refers to constitution number 86 in the OCSO Constitutions, and RB 72 refers to chapter 72 in the Rule of St. Benedict.

"The Order Needs Monks More Than Martyrs . . ."
(Tuesday, November 7, 1995)

You will recall the response that the abbot general, Father Bernardo, gave me at Timadeuc, in February last year, when I sought his counsel regarding what we had lived through: "The Order," he said, "needs MONKS more than martyrs. So you must do everything you can to avoid a tragic end that would benefit no one." He echoed the dread expressed by our bishop after the Christmas visit: "The hardest blow for everyone would be for you to suffer the same fate as the Croatians. We cannot afford [to lose you in that way]." Those two congruent words of caution express something that I believe to be profoundly true, and which is traditional in the Church (notably in the Church of Africa. See Saint Cyprian): We do not have the right to provoke death, including that of "martyrdom."

It would be wrong to put our neighbor into the immediate temptation of killing, by defying him directly on the ground where he stands, and where his blindness in the moment has confined him. However, that's not to say we should desert that ground. Besides, in most cases, it's not possible, except at the risk of being unfaithful to what we believe, to who we are, to what we have vowed, to the urgency of charity. Let us think of those who continue to care for people with contagious diseases. What to say about a Father Damien [of Molokai] who shut himself in with lepers?

In fact, we are still here, with the state of grace that enables us to say, "This is our place for the moment." We have not made an absolute choice. We will not stay "at any cost." In this situation we must remain faithful to our conscience, to our monastic ideal, to our environment, and to our Church. And that is why we found the remark made by Father Bernardo somewhat perplexing. It skirts the essential question, which is to know whether the Order needs us in this country, at this moment, whether our Church and our environment have need of us. The latter has told us so in many ways, and we rely on that. Our Church has too, in the support it offers us, and in its steadfast accompaniment of our discernment. We can say that Scripture also helps us on a daily basis. Just today, in Saint Paul to the Romans: "In times of tribulation, stand firm. Persevere in prayer" [11:11–12].

And our Order? Surely it is present. Surely it is wondering. It has always wondered about the meaning of our presence. Perhaps it is easier now to understand why we are here, like our brothers in Bosnia . . . ?

Cistercian Heritage
(Tuesday, December 12, 1995)

I said somewhat hastily that there were not many "martyrs" in the annals of the Order. Our contemporary era nonetheless provides us with some examples that the Church has recognized in varying degrees. There are the three brothers beatified on October 1 who died of exhaustion on the pontoons of Rochefort in 1794; two were from Sept-Fons and the other was a former prior of La Trappe. Other monks of the Order have died in "concentration camps," although their cause has not led anywhere. The process of our brothers from China is well advanced. We could ask Dom Armand, as postulator, to tell us where it stands. Some brothers were victims of persecution during Spain's dark years. And then there is the survivor of Akbès [Syria], crucified to the door of his monastery, which was destroyed during a revolt of the Druze.

For all those, and undoubtedly others whom it would be worth listing, there is a special place in what our Constitutions, in their preamble, call the "substantial spiritual heritage" of the Order, made up of "the lives and labors of innumerable brothers and sisters" that "found expression in writing, chant, architecture and crafts, and in the skillful management of their lands." This enumeration refers to daily life and to its multiple demands of "regular" beauty and creativity rather than to a witness of spilled blood, which could only be an exception. In that regard the monk seems no different from any other Christian (*a fortiori* from any other religious). He knows that his life does not belong to him, that it is definitively linked to the love of God that his faith inspires in him. He knows that the GIFT of his life is spent day by day, humbly, tenaciously. Because he wants to be a friend to all human beings, he cannot imagine a death [for himself] that would vilify any man, whoever he is, making him the murderer of his brother. If this should occur, God ALONE would provide the lamb for the sacrifice!

I was rereading an instruction of Saint Jane de Chantal to her daughters: "Neither Saint Basil nor most of our holy Fathers and pillars of the Church were martyred. Why? I believe it is because there is a martyrdom called the *Martyrdom of love* through which God, sustaining the lives of his servants, men and women, that they may work for His glory, renders them martyrs and confessors at the same time."

A "CONSTANCY" of Love [*amour*]
(Thursday, December 14, 1995)

Saint Jane de Chantal was then asked how long this "martyrdom" would last. Her response: "From the moment we give ourselves to God unreservedly until the moment of our death. However, this has to be understood in relation to generous hearts that, without holding anything back, are faithful to love. As for those with weaker hearts and little love or constancy, Our Lord does not bother with tormenting them. He is content to let them go their own way, lest they shun him, because he never violates our free will." She adds: "Love is as MAD as death, and the martyrs of love suffer a thousand times more by staying alive to do the will of God than if they had to give a thousand lives in witness of their faith, love, and fidelity."

We can appreciate the wisdom of her language. It's not inviting us to some mediocre life. It judges us. We're inclined to move at a slow pace, winding on the back roads. But we could say perhaps that for the past two years we have especially been in a hurry to keep up the pace and, more than that, to understand the folly that is common to love and death. By risking one, we risk the other. However, even in this great state of urgency, we so easily find ourselves holding back!

I can still hear the response of the Cardinal [Duval] after Christmas '93. "What is your advice?" His answer: "CONSTANCY. . . ." The very thing that Saint Jane de Chantal (a Savoyard herself!) identifies with hearts that are strong. It's thus a matter of HOLDING ON and holding on TOGETHER: *cum-stare*, like the city of God where "all together make one BODY" [Ps 122:3]. Therein is a first note of the STABILITY that we permanently vowed to each other: constancy in the place and constancy with the brothers, love of the place and love of the brothers, *amator loci et fratrum*, according to Benedict's definition of a monk, as transmitted by Saint Gregory. With the nuance that events have added to our charism: this place has other inhabitants who are also our brothers in constancy in this difficult day-to-day.

We are tied, at least for the moment and by mutual consent, to the happiness of peace for which the people surrounding us are unceasingly hoping for the entire country. [They express that hope] in particular by continuing to make a place for us, thus refusing to identify themselves with an Algeria that would expel foreigners or an Islam that would execute non-Muslims. It's been two years to the day since this concern became more acute for us following the horror of Tamesguida. Our stability and its constancy honor the spontaneous behavior of most of our neighbors. The risk that we have undertaken is also a witness (martyrdom) offered to their rejection of violence and bloodshed.

Christmas . . . and Us
(Thursday January 4, 1996)

To what has been said about our Constitutions, we should add a similar observation from the *Ratio* for formation. No explicit evocation of the mystery of the Incarnation itself. In the paragraph on formation through WORK it is written: "Through work, especially manual work, monks and nuns joyfully participate in the CREATIVE activity of the Father and live in communion with all workers, especially the poor. Their work, which can sometimes be an experience of fatigue, tension, or frustration, is a participation in the CROSS of Christ. . . ."

No mention of the school of Nazareth which would allow us to decipher, over more than thirty years of Jesus's life, the constant interpenetration of the mysteries of the Incarnation and the Redemption. The latter is always more readily mentioned, even though it is somehow subordinate to the former in the order of succession and of revelation in time. As for us, I strongly agree with what Gilles (Nicolas) told us in his Christmas homily where he probed the mystery of the Incarnation for the true rooting of our reasons for "staying" despite the threats and the turmoil. In a letter to his loved ones, he emphasizes: "Christmas is EMMANUEL, God silently present, but the presence of Love which alone is revolutionary, which alone transforms hearts, those of each other." And he adds, which is relevant to us: "That the Eucharist is celebrated on this mountain of TIBHIRINE populated by rough and simple people, attached to Islam and attached to 'their' monks, seems to me to have a very important meaning, and not just symbolic."

In fact, I believe it is much healthier psychologically and mentally, and also in closer conformity to the monastic tradition, for those of us living this situation to take on the imitation of CHRIST as an offering of the Incarnation continued through "the humble consecration of 'a hidden life' of prayer and work" (expression of *Perfectae Caritatis* 9), rather than by associating it directly and solely with the CROSS and martyrdom, isolated from their concrete context of a long-shared life. The presence of Mary at Calvary indicates that what was experienced for a long time in the familial intimacy of Nazareth (in the broad sense) continues.

To the quip of our abbot general saying that our Order needs monks more than martyrs, we must therefore respond that we are truly monks by continuing to live here the very mystery of Christmas, of GOD LIVING with men . . . and thereby exposing himself, from the cradle, to the massacre of the Innocents—as if to better signify that prior to the Cross there were crowds of innocent people massacred, just as there have been crowds since, and around us. We will never again be able to forget that our direct confrontation with the grave misfortune that struck the country took place in this liturgical context, between the night of December 14 and that of December 24.

The Communitarian Character of the INCARNATION (Tuesday, January 30, 1996— after the Regular Visit from January 11 to January 20)

(The reading at Vigils tonight picks up where we left off with *Gaudium et Spes*. One of the last issues of *La Croix* we received—but from December 4!—stressed the importance of this document, which is now thirty years old, [Jesus's] age at Nazareth! See also the gift from Gilles Nicolas: the three cassettes of Fr. Varillon on the Incarnation.)

In *Gaudium et Spes* 32, we touch on the theme of the next General Chapter, since the text underscores the COMMUNITARIAN character of all of salvation history manifested in all the deeds and gestures of the Incarnate Word. "He sanctified human ties. . . . He willingly obeyed the laws of his country. He chose to live the life proper to an artisan of his time and place. In his preaching, he clearly taught the sons of God to treat one another as brothers. In his prayers, he pleaded that all his disciples might be 'one.' . . . He offered himself for ALL. . . . He commanded his apostles to preach to all peoples the Gospel's message," etc. And number 38 takes up the same teaching by grounding all this activity in the commandment of LOVE, whose "way lies open to ALL men." It is through the sharing of everyday life that one can experience the "universal fraternity" that demands that man dedicate all his efforts to one legitimate and ultimate end. This charity is not first and foremost the fruit of a few heroic actions; rather it is above all "in daily life" that it is exercised (the Council insists!).

"To give one's life for those we love" [Jn 15:13] is not an isolated act that requires a quest for martyrdom or that, in the case of Jesus, is identified [exclusively] with the supreme gift consummated on Calvary. Jesus taught us that the CROSS is "daily," and that is the characteristic that lends its price and its weight "to all the works in favor of justice and peace" [GS 38]. What takes place during the hours of the Passion is the Incarnation continued: the Word [*Verbe*] takes on flesh and human texture just as much as in the days of his birth and growing up. He came to inhabit suffering and death as well as all the other realities shared by the people of this world in order to bring to completion the great dynamism of Incarnation, rooted in the glory that he received from his Father from the very beginning. The very fulfillment of Redemption is this Incarnation of a humanity similar to ours in the glory of God . . . and, at the same time, the entrance of God into the human community through the communion of saints.

CST 86: "They JOYFULLY Make Their Way . . ." (Thursday, February 1, 1996)

I propose to search with you for traces of the "Paschal mystery" in the Cistercian charism . . . allowing ourselves to be drawn into a meditation on the mystery of the Incarnation, perhaps discovering even more the extent to which the Incarnate Word [*Verbe*] represents the specificity of the Christian message. The times of Advent and Christmas make this approach all the more relevant. Traditionally the feast tomorrow marks the completion of forty days after the Nativity. We figured we had unpacked the "joyful mysteries" and, with Lent already so close, that we would be ready to move on to the "sorrowful mysteries," which seem to communicate the true makeup of the mission of Christ, who comes to heal and save all people by the blood of the Cross.

That second forty-day period has always weighed heavily in our approach to the "Paschal mystery," much more so it seems, in certain eras, than the last forty-day period, between Easter and the Ascension, which is intended to familiarize us with the "glorious mysteries." However, unpacking the traditional mysteries of the ROSARY with Mary, how can we not be seized by their mutual interpenetrations, their constant resonance with each other? The Cross and Glory are fully present in the Joy that Simeon and Anna express. And that [combination] is what truly signifies the Incarnate Word [*Verbe*]. It is also what fulfills his mission to SAVE, to REDEEM all people by teaching them to taste this new blend of joy and suffering, of death and life, by which humanity can satisfy its deepest thirst, that of God forever.

That is why it is necessary to observe that the Paschal mystery is co-extensive with that of the Incarnation, that is to say with human LIFE and vice-versa. Jesus teaches us that [life] has a vocation to eternity, including, and perhaps especially, in its passage through (bodily) death. In the *Pascha* of Christ, Incarnation is the mode, Redemption is the motive. The Cross is part of the mode; it does not exhaust the motive. The [Church] Fathers used to say, by way of an image, that the cradle is already the cross where the Son will be laid down. They also said that the Cross is like the cradle of the firstborn among the dead. It seems to me that the final Constitution, number 86, confirms this by inviting us to "joyfully make our way to the fullness of love" (what David would call: "going the way of all the earth" in 1 Kgs 2:2, today!).

And DEATH, Is It a Question?
(Tuesday, February 13, 1996)

It's about "remaining on earth," keeping our feet on the ground, all while aiming for the "heavens," not losing sight of the objective, the end: the tops of trees do not turn back on their roots. There is no reason we should escape this law of creation, which yearns for "what is above" [Col 3:2]. It's for us to choose that orientation freely, from a constantly renewed desire, the sap of which irrigates all our impulses without ceasing to be drawn from the soil of everyday life. The tree of the cross allows this comparison. All the dimensions of man are revealed there, from the vertical, to the horizontal outstretched arms. And if we find ourselves continually contemplating it, it is because the true CROSS is not the piece of wood that kills, but this tree of life in every way like us, whose head touches the sky and where everyone can find their nest in the gash of an open heart.

Because the Incarnation of the Son of God, in full communion with humanity, passed through death, the meaning of our death now changes. It is not the site of disintegration. It is no longer an uprooting, but a definitive rooting where it's the head that has taken root. The great movement of the Incarnation is that of Jacob's ladder, where we never cease descending and ascending in order to embrace everything about the human condition that finds fulfillment in this "spiritual ardor": it would be death not to hang on to the rungs, whether the first or the very last!

So, is DEATH a question in our Constitutions? Violent death in particular? We have said: martyrdom, "dying for the faith," is not envisaged there. Is that because the monk must avoid it, or never be exposed to it? Perhaps it is because it adds nothing substantial to the dynamism of Incarnation that nourishes and confirms his consecration. It is of the same nature as that violence that we must sometimes impose upon ourselves through simple fidelity to ordinary things. That is, what we evoked (Michel) when speaking about our successive "departures": family, country, etc. And then, we have said, no one should seek [violent death], or even desire it as such. It can only come to us in the logic of a continuous desire for LIFE. So our Constitutions get it right when they speak of death almost "accidentally." For example, in Constitution 8 (Monastic Consecration): "The brother binds himself in faithful stability to a sincere conversion of LIFE through ready obedience until DEATH."

And the Other Congregations Represented Here?
(Saturday, February 17, 1996)

It is neither a question of "martyrdom" nor of violent death, nor even of "giving one's life" in the classical and "realistic" meaning of the term in our Constitutions. The only violence mentioned is that which we choose to impose on our own will. Those who have practiced it know that that is indeed a true "martyrdom," colloquially speaking. It is the greater JIHAD, the true struggle of which the spiritual tradition of Islam speaks. Today, let us explore the responses of some of the other religious families represented in Algeria in order to paint a clearer picture, according to the charisms of these congregations, of what we are currently living here. It is something that Bishop [Francisco Javier] Errázuriz already broached with the Sisters of Our Lady of the Apostles.

The White Sisters quote their Constitution 9: "The charity of Christ compels us. . . . It leads us to be all things to all people, not shrinking from any suffering, even death, in order to continue expanding the Kingdom of God." They include citations from Cardinal Lavigerie (1867): "It is probably nicer to live in Lyon, but it is certainly less hard to live [as a Christian] in Algiers, especially if, as I am assured, there is much to suffer there" (referring to Staouëli?). Additionally, several texts from their Constitutions, or minutes from their recent regional chapters, speak of involvement in situations of distress, closeness to a suffering people, and strength through patience in predicaments without a solution. . . . The Little Sisters [of Jesus] (Oran) quote from their Constitutions: "Immersed in suffering with our people, and touched to the depth of our being, it is there that we meet God, who preceded us and who comes to deliver us into weakness, poverty, and the cross. The resurrection of Jesus, the source from which life springs . . . nourishes the hope of the Little Sisters in situations where death seems to win." They also cite the green notebook of Little Sister Magdalene: "You must not shrink from any danger, while accepting the risk of violent death." The Little Brothers [of Jesus]: their response is simply a series of extracts from their Constitutions: "The Holy Spirit teaches them to love to the point of giving their life for Jesus and for their brothers. . . . They may perhaps have to suffer persecution (37). Like Jesus, they take the path of nonviolence (92). If it happens that they are misunderstood, rejected, or persecuted, they will recall the words of the Lord: 'Love your enemies and pray for them.' They refrain from all violence toward anyone, praying to

God to be able to follow their Master to the end, in the gift of their blood, should this supreme proof of love be asked of them (93)." They conclude with: "It is understandable that no brother has left, especially from the country where Father de Foucauld gave his life."

However, Brother Bruno rejoins that that's not the essential point, for "if I surrender my body to the flames but do not have love, I am NOTHING" [1 Cor 13:3].

Untitled
(Thursday, March 14, 1996)

(Continued: homily) The Trinitarian environment as a "school" of CHARITY. We can speak of a SCHOOL in God in the sense that each Person must receive from the other, to learn from the Other who they are. Where there is CHARITY, there is necessarily a "school."

Of Good ZEAL . . . RB 72
(Saturday, March 16, 1996)

After the preamble on CONTEMPLATION-CHARITY, a veritable SCHOOL. . . . It seems quite natural to return to the school of Saint Benedict, the "master to whom we have lent something of our inner ear," so that he can educate us in the contemplative life and the life of charity.

From its Prologue, as we know, the *Rule* explains the project it is pursuing: "We want to found a SCHOOL where we serve the Lord (*Dominici SCOLA servitii*)." This is the only use of the word "SCHOOL." Shortly after, the word *CARITAS* is added . . . , which seems to mark the culmination of the Prologue and therefore the ultimate goal of the entire *Rule* and the Benedictine school that it defines: CHARITY, DILECTION, DILATION of the heart . . . all in the PATIENCE of stability and perseverance, our way of "participating in the sufferings of Christ," our "MARTYRDOM," which must therefore be a *martyrdom of love*, and just as much a *martyrdom of HOPE* since everything in this passage is in motion, walking, running toward the Kingdom of which the community is the image, though not yet the full reality.

Most commentators on the *Rule* have observed a parallel between the Prologue (particularly its conclusion) and, at the other end, the chapter on GOOD ZEAL, *zelum bonum*. It is this chapter that we will try to RE-READ together, always in the perspective of the theme of the General Chapter, not directly to prepare for the General Chapter, but to let ourselves be drawn on a daily basis in the direction that it traces for us and which says EVERYTHING, in fact, about what we want to be.

Of course, it was the letter from the abbot general that aroused my curiosity and my appreciation for this very small chapter of our *Rule*, where everything is stated so naturally and simply that one could read it as just a list of foregone conclusions. We sometimes approach the BEATITUDES in the same way, that is, as if they were an everyday thing, as if our life had only an [everyday] language for making sense of itself. It occurs to me that there are as many "NOTES" of "good zeal" as there are BEATITUDES: EIGHT; as many as the harmonics in a range going from DO to DO, precisely an octave. Let's just read the whole passage . . .

Letters

Maurice Borrmans (1925–2017) was a professor at the Pontifical Institute for the Study of Arabic and Islam (PISAI) when de Chergé was a student there and for many years after that. He enjoyed an important teaching ministry and served as director of studies. He also published a number of works on the Qur'an, Islamic law, and the Catholic approach to Islam. From its founding until he retired in 2004, he was the editor of Islamochristiana, *PISAI's academic journal. As mentioned in the introduction, Christian de Chergé kept up a voluminous correspondence with many people, but for the moment the letters to Borrmans are the only ones to have been published as a stand-alone collection. We translated nine letters, or in some cases extracts of letters, that offer windows onto the affectionate nature of the two men's friendship, the impatience that occasionally accompanies de Chergé's positive attitude toward Islam, and the differences in the approaches to dialogue with Muslims between the former teacher and pupil. Also, more strongly and more personally than in his studies and talks, de Chergé's Eucharistic devotion emerges in these letters to dearest Maurice.*

From Christian de Chergé, *Lettres à un ami fraternel*, ed. Maurice Borrmans (Montrouge, France: Bayard Éditions, 2015).

Tibhirine, September 26, 1979

Dearest Maurice,

Your feast day was not so long ago [Memorial of St. Maurice, September 22]. It remains fitting to tell you how much I united myself with you and all your intentions on the occasion, my celebration of the Eucharist echoing yours. I love these relays of affection that span the distances and deceive absence into welcoming a Presence where we know we will find ourselves close and alive, all the more united as we mysteriously commune beyond our current pilgrimage. The Eucharist is for me the profound moment of answering all the questions of our human divergences, especially our shared existence with the believers of Islam who join the communion of all the saints by another path.

One may be inclined to seek in the daily life of Muslims the Eucharistic trace of this shared vocation to the Reality that transcends the sacrament. How does the Spirit, who works on hearts, fashion, in the very expression of faith, this Eucharistic countenance, where man finds his perfection ever since Christ offered it to us? That is—*grosso modo*—the theme of our meditation leading up to the next gathering of the small informal group I mentioned to you. Our bond, over these next six months, is to gaze with faith upon everything that lives here, the better to discern the hidden dimensions of thanksgiving and selflessness. At the same time we will try to discover what that means in the Qur'an.

I strongly believe that there can be a profound dialogue with the "people of Islam" that starts from this radical—and theological in the strongest sense—orientation that connects them with so many who have gone before us, marked even in their death by the sign of their respective faith. It is up to us to incarnate this reality of the Kingdom—[the saints'] communion of glory in the total surrender of the Son—by realizing all the potential complementarities of our faithfulness to God. Moreover, one would think that the God "who calls us to prayer," both of us, becomes impatient in seeing how little inclined we are to correspond, that is, to "respond together."

Those who dare this correspondence perceive better, and with such joy, how personal faith alone is alive, and that it is quite impossible to express it in the manner of the anathemas we have been hurling at each other for centuries. It is not about relativizing dogma, but rather about our understanding of the dogma, which is a completely different matter. Such a spiritual adventure reveals the concordances: "It is the secret of God's love, *sirr al-mahabba*," that unites us, "as was recently told to me by a neighboring mufti whose wisdom is respected throughout the country" (see the article by Juguet in *Études*, August–September, and also the latest issue of *Spiritus*).

Obviously I stammer ... and you furrow your brows. In the end, God knows best, and this certainty reassures and delights me. Still, it is impossible not to share with you something of this challenging step-by-step that admittedly questions so many simplistic and reductionist formulations. The other calls me to see God and His Christ as greater. What a marvel, this presence that encounters me while challenging me.

...

I entrust myself to your prayer, and I assure you of my own lowly prayer, with an abundance of gratitude and affection, *in Christo*.

Br. Christian

The attachment to which de Chergé refers in the following letter is a comparative study of the notion and functions of mercy in the Islamic and Christian traditions that he would publish in 1983 as "Let Us Come to a Common Word: Christians and Muslims, Witnesses and Pilgrims of Mercy." It is a close reading of John Paul II's encyclical Dives in Misericordia *(1980), in point-by-point conversation with passages from the Qur'an. The study is published in Christian de Chergé,* L'invincible espérance, *ed. Bruno Chenu (Montrouge, France: Bayard Éditions, 2010), 67–108.*

Tibhirine, February 21, 1981

Dearest Maurice,

. . .

I am attaching the first part of an approach to Mercy in the Qur'an in response to the recent encyclical. I admit to having been very "shocked" not to find in the message of John Paul II any allusion, even implicit, to what remains central, "nuclear," in the faith of Muslims. It's a "lapse" that I won't try too hard to make sense of or to justify. Because even if the Pope is free to address only Christians, is it possible to speak in a Christian manner about Mercy without doing justice to all its "keys" in the hearts and religious traditions of humanity?

It seems that the Secretariat for Non-Christians has the absolutely necessary task of providing information to the Pope himself, who cannot be reproached for being a bit less encyclopedic than he appears. I am sure that this connection with Islam has escaped him. But is anyone in Rome aware that no Muslim can read the Encyclical without feeling deeply ignored and without us feeling, once again, splendidly certain of being the only ones to have and know everything?

This criticism that we often direct to them [in Rome],

and rightfully so in many instances . . . is like a dialogue with the deaf. The least we could say is that mercy-in-action requires an entirely different kind of listening. In this sense, we find passages in the Qur'an that are quite moving.

. . .

As we head toward a new *Pascha*, I embrace you most affectionately,

Christian

The Fatihâ, *mentioned in the following letter, is the opening chapter* (sura) *and prayer of the Qur'an. It is ubiquitous in Muslim devotional life, recited at every formal prayer but also at almost any significant occasion, including weddings, births, business arrangements, lectures, and so on. The testimony to which de Chergé refers is "Praying in the Church. Listening to Islam." It is included in the section of articles at the end of this collection. The "Catho" is a nickname for the Institut catholique de Paris.*

Tibhirine, June 12, 1982

Dearest Maurice,

. . .

I will carefully read the texts you provided. It's all the more striking since I recently came across a commentary on the *Fatihâ* that was completely opposite, and in my view much closer to the Qur'anic tradition. We shouldn't confine ourselves to the commentaries that have been approved up to now, as it seems to me that we'll increasingly seek other references. You yourself have witnessed the unexpected relativization of Thomism, and so many other exegetical stances adopted by the Church for a long time to the exclusion of all others.

I'm sharing with you the testimony that was requested of me, that of the place of Islam in a spiritual journey. I did not want to enter into a pointless polemic. But I believe with all my heart that to truly engage in dialogue, we must accept, in the name of Christ, that Islam has something to tell us on behalf of Christ. Otherwise, everyone stays in their own world, and the polite attention we show to the other remains unproductive, except to help us provide apologetic arguments.

I recently read the testimony of a priest, a convert from Judaism and a professor at "the Catho," who longed for a Church whose catholicity would be enriched by openness and listening, such that the Spirit at work in Judaism could express itself freely.

In all of this, it is natural to fumble. I am sure you could be called upon to play a valuable role in such fumbling in the dark.

With all my deep affection, and my thanks,

Christian

De Chergé's attachment to the Alawiyya Sufi community highlights a tension in the approaches to dialogue between Borrmans, who focused on the juridical traditions of Islam, and de Chergé, who concentrated on the spiritual traditions. For a description of the Ribât, *which is mentioned by de Chergé in the following letter, see the introduction to the collection.* Se comprendre *(Understanding Each Other) was a bulletin published at PISAI and edited by Borrmans. The publication in* Lettre de Ligugé *is the article on Christian and Muslim understandings of mercy mentioned in a previous letter. SRI stands for Service for Relations with Islam, which was an advisory committee to the Catholic bishops of France. Jean-Marie Le Pen (b. 1928) was president of the French far-right National Front political party, which advocated for strict anti-immigration policies. Marcel Lefebvre (1905–1991) was the Catholic bishop of Tulle, France. Critical of the Second Vatican Council, especially its teaching on religious liberty and positive regard for non-Christians, he founded a "traditional" seminary in Switzerland. He was excommunicated in 1988 when, against the explicit warning of Pope John Paul II, he illicitly ordained four bishops.* Dâr al-Islâm *means the* House of Islam; *it refers to territories that are religiously and juridically governed by Islam.*

Tibhirine, February 25, 1985

Dearest Maurice,

Your letter of January 20th arrived after I'd left, and I only found it upon my return last Wednesday. I have just returned from a short monastic tour, interspersed with a week in Paris and some family time; I was attending a meeting of superiors from the "Region," which was held at Timadeuc (Brittany). Before that, I spent a week at Aiguebelle and got to live in a community different from my own, something I hadn't done for ten years. This tour of our [monastic] families was necessary for discerning the changes and also, I believe, to put a human face on our existence. In Paris, I established good contact with Michel Serain from SRI and also with the "grand sheikh" of the Alawiyya in Drancy. Despite the disastrous political climate toward immigrants, I was fortunate to witness some small details of life, in the street, on the train, or on the boat, where North Africans who seemed a bit lost were treated with genuine affability. Le Pen still isn't the Gospel.

. . .

Thank you for this excellent letter with which I "correspond" completely, as it seems very attentive to all the forms of welcoming Islam (i.e., Muslims) and eager to interpret each in its own context and according to various concrete situations. Thank you for being respectful of the "smoldering wick" . . . and for believing that there is a certain spiritual approach to Islam among a minority of Muslims that it would be detrimental to hide, if only because its calling indeed may be to illuminate the entire "house" (*Dâr al-Islâm!*). I will, therefore, tend the flame, as you wish, while remaining aware—and sometimes feeling really and deeply *torn*—of what can be pretty widely committed, or said, or believed, in the name of a hard and undeniably combative Islam. I say simply that this is not the Islam of God . . . no more than Le Pen or Archbishop Lefebvre can claim to embody the Gospel in my eyes. I believe that the *Ribât* in a sense launches a challenge against generalizations that are too easy and that reduce hope (and therefore reality). You will certainly have received the mini-journal (no. 2) composed by Claude [Rault]. Our next meeting is at the end of March on the theme of the *trial* (remember the *hadiths* collected by Ghazâlî).

Go figure that my article in the *Lettre de Ligugé* received an unexpected welcome among the monks, and even more so with the nuns (here and there, it's read in the refectory!). It seems a little long for *Se comprendre* . . . although I believe it aligns with the title of the journal. I must find the time to write the next article, which will focus on fraternal love. So thank you, again and again, for remaining the older brother, eager to understand even the impossible, in the name of the universal whose call and wound he carries. I join you on this paschal journey in the one who delivers us, with him, alive to the multitude.

Affectionately,

Christian

The article under discussion in the following letter is "Christians and Muslims: Do Our Differences Mean Communion?," published in Christian de Chergé, L'invincible espérance, ed. Bruno Chenu (Montrouge, France: Bayard Éditions, 2010), 109–66. In that article, as the title implies, de Chergé develops both the idea of difference as a quasi sacrament of union and also the idea that Christians and Muslims, eschatologically, are oriented toward a mysterious unity in God, a unity we glimpse here and now in what de Chergé refers to as the communion of saints, and which includes both Christians and Muslims. Readers can infer Borrmans's critiques of the article: too confident about Christian–Muslim communion, insufficiently attentive to difference, insufficiently theological, too Sufi. The Journées romaines, *Roman Days, was an annual meeting hosted by PISAI for Catholic missionaries living and working in Muslim-majority societies.*

Tibhirine, June 26, 1985

Dearest Maurice,

It's already been a month since I received your long letter. The season isn't really conducive to correspondence, but I must thank you for taking the time out of your busy schedule for this fraternal sharing.

. . .

Your summer seems to be quite challenging, with being torn between Rome and Bahrain, not to mention the other travels and places. Take care of your health. Also, take the time to read and listen. Everything happens so fast. There are so many initiatives here and there. In all of this, there must always be a tangible sign of the already realized communion in Christ, and already given in the Church. Though the Church has only us to manifest itself.

On this subject, have you read the paper by Archbishop

[Angelo] Fernandes [of New Delhi]: "Calls for Dialogue with Non-Christians," in *Documentation catholique* (no. 1887)? Clear applications for where we are. A beautiful testimony of a theology that is being developed. Indeed, I think with Father [Youakim] Moubarac that we have not yet researched much in this area, except for a few exceptions that are hardly noticed. We will always be "in diapers" as long as we, of our own doing, set boundaries to the Kingdom.

As you might imagine, I read, pencil in hand, your "free reflections" on my free musings. I haven't had time to copy what I noted spontaneously, while comparing what I wrote and what you read. I regret not being more explicit here and there. But the only concession I would make to you is not putting the *Word* [*Verbe*] between " " when I use the term, as many others do, regarding the Qur'anic "Word" [*Verbe coranique*].

Your observations are numerous on the first pages . . . which pose the problem, and almost nonexistent on the last ones . . . which are supposed to provide answers *primo motu* to your criticisms at the beginning. It would be easier to come back to this when we're face to face. But it is certain that without an eschatological vision of Christianity, and therefore a mystical one of man and his future, one can only trip over what I write . . . and continue to trip over the Muslim *fact*. Christ is the Gatherer of the last day; that's my faith . . . and the Church is only the imperfect sign (in what is visible) of this perfect reality, but the object of experience.

Curious! Some Muslim friends reproached me for having too much theology in that article when it would be so much easier to talk about communion, purely and simply, which shows how often we stammer, both them and us, in similar ways.

As for the Alawiyya confraternity, it deserves to exist. I do not believe it is monistic, judging by the brothers with whom we are in contact. To see God in everything and in everyone is purely and simply the vocation of a monk (or will we say it is "monistic" because it takes its name from "monos"?). In fact, monks are as rare in Christianity as the Alawiyya and their colleagues are in Islam . . . forerunners, both here and there, no doubt destined to know each other better because they are so drawn to each other by their "magnetic poles."

I was a bit sad, moreover, because of your insistent suggestion to "listen to your brothers." I must ask: Which ones?

The next article for *Lettre de Ligugé* will focus on fraternal love . . . if I have time to rewrite my notes. I recently received two issues of *Se comprendre*. I can still detect you in this dispatch. I can never thank you enough for all the tenderness shown toward me and vis-à-vis the community. I think you must have received, on your end, the two issues of *Ribât*.

We are preparing our shared retreat: "Blessed are the strangers" is the chosen theme . . . too bad Claude is taken away by the *Journées romaines*.

Have a good summer. With all my fraternal gratitude and my deep affection (the heart has reasons that reason doesn't know!).

Christian

In the following letter de Chergé regrets not having been able to spend more time with Borrmans at the 1989 meeting of the Journées romaines *mentioned in the previous letter. De Chergé had given a talk, "The Mystical Ladder of Dialogue," later published, and now translated for this collection. The Esslimani mentioned is Sheikh Hocine Esslimani, the Algerian Islamic scholar who would participate in the 1995 "Sant'Egidio platform" peace negotiations.* Islamochristiana *was a second and more academically oriented journal, along with* Se comprendre, *sponsored by PISAI and edited by Maurice Borrmans. Whereas* Se comprendre *ceased being published in 2013,* Islamochristiana *continues to this day. Here readers also get a taste of de Chergé's occasional biting and sarcastic wit, especially as directed toward authority figures.*

Tibhirine, September 22, 1989

Dearest Maurice,

On the day of your feast, my prayer has flown to you, and from you to Him, trying to take with it your intentions, your wishes, your fears. I even allowed myself to add a wish: that you may be fully freed from your fear, and that you may blossom in charity, more and more living out all that you have accumulated, over the years, of knowledge and relationships. It is a marvel to rely on the One who knows the depths of hearts and who constantly invites us to share His feast with each other in the "secret point of the encounter": *nuqtat al-liqâ'* (as a cousin of Esslimani called it recently, acknowledging that it exists in *every* man).

I deeply regretted that you disappeared so quickly. I would like to have heard your immediate reactions and to have returned with you to our conversation of the previous evening. There is also the response to your question left pending . . . in fact, it seems to me that I had already given you the answer. What I feel, from experience, is that the simple people—Christians or Muslims—have intuitions that we need not fear too much will cause confusion. Such intuitions usually tend in the direction of communion by way of shortcuts that only rarely violate the respect due to the other.

I would also like to have discussed with you the audience at Castel Gandolfo, which disappointed me. Not the

Holy Father [John Paul II] himself. . . . Could we expect him to know everything about us and to have the right words in the moment? But the one who prepared the speech seems to me to be in a state of "grave sin"! For two reasons:

- a single reference to *Nostra Aetate* (twice), without any support from the Pope's many speeches which have greatly advanced our approach to Muslims (thus a sin of ignorance . . . or refusal?)
- the theme of the *Journées romaines* was addressed, but there was no reference to the people present and belonging to almost all the countries visited by the Pope, from the Philippines to Morocco . . . no mention of Lebanon represented by Father [Samir Khalil] Samir [SJ]. As if the Pope were forbidden from having in Rome the direct relationships he proliferates elsewhere. This lack of understanding of people seems to me—alas!—even more serious than the other. I add the absence of Assisi. Yikes! It's a lot. . . . If you know the *"de cujus,"* you can pay him my compliments. On the other hand, he writes well!

That said, I hope your stay in Turkey was fruitful. Good luck on the return to PISAI and for publishing the new edition of *Islamochristiana*. Thanks for all you do.
. . .
Everything is fine here, day to day. Tomorrow? God is the master of the clouds! I embrace you with all my gratitude and affection,

Christian

The IPEA—the Pontifical Institute for Arabic Studies—was the predecessor to PISAI. The two religious families that descend from Charles Cardinal Lavigerie (1825–1892) are the Missionaries of

Africa, or White Fathers, to which Maurice Borrmans belonged, and the Missionary Sisters of Our Lady of Africa, or White Sisters.

Tibhirine, November 30, 1992

Dearest Maurice,

I don't remember whether I responded to your Saint Bernard's Day letter, which as always was so faithful and affectionate. It seems to me that I did so from France, where we had a meeting at the end of August, but I thought of you, that's for sure, on the feast of Saint Maurice. And [I've thought of you] often in recent days: twenty years already since I cut my teeth at the former "IPEA"! It's a good opportunity to thank you again for your patience then and since. Thursday, I participated in the closing celebration of the year of Lavigerie at Notre-Dame d'Afrique. I met Gérard Demeerseman there. There was a fairly good turnout. I wanted to convey the forgiveness of "La Trappe" to an archbishop who so seriously mistreated our brothers of Staouëli in relation to financial concerns . . . and also our gratitude for the two religious families descended from him. In the refectory we are reading the biography of the cardinal by Fr. Renault.

These days, I find that a lot of very "timid" articles are being published on relations between Christians and Muslims. The Holy Spirit must not really know how to escape from the cage in which he is confined. . . . I very much don't like a theology that excludes in advance the possibility for the centurion Cornelius to have an authentic spiritual experience! Does *Se comprendre* share in this retreat?

I am also writing to you to find out if the PISAI bookstore still has [Khalil] Gibran's *The Prophet* in Arabic? If so, I would love to have two copies, but we'll have to wait for more certain circumstances. The postal service these days. . . .

Here we are once again engaged in the same [Advent] waiting. In advance, I wish you a Merry Christmas and a fruitful year. As a brother,

Christian

From the Introduction, readers are familiar with the events of Christmas Eve 1993, presented in the following letter with a beautiful reflection on the meaning of Emmanuel. Michael Fitzgerald (b. 1937), a White Father like Maurice Borrmans and a specialist in Islam, was eventually ordained a bishop and became the president of the Pontifical Council for Interreligious Dialogue (2002–2006). Pope Francis created Fitzgerald a cardinal in 2019. Sr. Anne-Marie Blanc was a White Sister and collaborator with Maurice Borrmans and Christian de Chergé on various publications.

Tibhirine, Beginning of 1994

Dear Maurice,

I'm late, and these wishes are already dated. It is because there was the unexpected Christmas . . . which began, for us, with the horrible "massacre of the innocents" at Tamesguida (4 km away as the crow flies). We knew these Croatian friends, our faithful companions on Christmas and Easter nights. Suddenly, everyone was interested in us . . . and that gave us an unsettling Christmas night . . . but the Child, in the depths of the night, was not surprised. We welcomed him as Emmanuel: He was with *us* . . . and, little by little, we accepted that he could ask us to remain *with*, like him. And it's more or less going okay . . . even if, momentarily, we had to reduce the community.

Send my best wishes to those around you, especially to Mike Fitzgerald. I was so sorry not to be able to see or hear Anne-Christine! The telephone in Saint-Charles was broken . . . and we were really stuck there, me at least. This is the second time this has happened. Pity! I hope at least that you were able to talk at length.

With my thanks for your long fidelity, I again entrust *us* to your prayer and assure you of my very fraternal and affectionate communion.

Christian

In the following letter, de Chergé writes from his monastery's annex at Fez, Morocco, where the monks who avoided the March 27, 1996, kidnapping would eventually relocate. Sant'Egidio is an Italian Catholic lay association founded in 1968, known in part for its work in interreligious dialogue and peacebuilding. During the Algerian civil war, representatives attempted, unsuccessfully, to broker a peace agreement between the warring parties. Several members of Sant'Egidio were close to the monks of Tibhirine. Sr. Odette Prévost (1932–1995) was a Little Sister of the Sacred Heart. She was a librarian in Algiers, where she was assassinated on her way to mass just a few weeks before Christian sent this postcard to Borrmans, November 10, 1995. She is among the nineteen martyrs of the Algerian civil war beatified by Pope Francis in 2018. Given the tragedies he had witnessed, the hope that Christian expresses for Algeria in this note is extraordinary. In this collection we have included the talk de Chergé delivered at an annual meeting of Monastic Interreligious Dialogue, "Intermonastic Dialogue and Islam."

Fez [Morocco], November 28, 1995

Dear Maurice,

The boy and the little girl [on the front of the postcard], in the same boat, on the sand, perhaps represent the image of tomorrow's Algeria, with a smile regained, and Peace imagined as a new distribution in a pluralistic society. No one can deny the indisputable characteristics of the recent presidential election: very strong participation / courage of the people / victory of women / determination against armed violence / option for a moderate and pluralist Islam / failure of the call for boycott as well as the "grand parties" that the platform of "Sant'Egidio" was supposed to create. . . . Of course, insecurity remains . . . but this childlike hope must be given time to grow. So much suffering has contributed to its birth, right up to the blood of Odette, maternally offered. I attach the outline of an interview given to DIM (Monastic Interreligious Dialogue) meant to awaken the monastic conscience to the perspectives of a specific dialogue with the Islamic world (and not only Sufi!).

Merry Christmas and Happy New Year!

Christian

Retreat

As a monk and a priest, Christian de Chergé was sometimes called upon to preach retreats, whether to groups visiting Notre Dame de l'Atlas or in other locations. On November 18–25, 1990, he led a retreat for the Little Sisters of Jesus in Mohammedia, Morocco. As the theme for the week, de Chergé commented on several texts from the biblical Song of Songs, which he paired with the letters to the churches in the Book of Revelation. Among de Chergé's goals was to have the sisters appropriate for themselves the love story at the heart of the Song of Songs, allegorically interpreted as the soul's relationship to God. At the fourth session of the retreat, de Chergé interjects the biblical story of Mary's visitation to Elizabeth (Lk 1:39–56). He comments on the narrative and attaches his own story of dialogue with a local Muslim friend in which together they "dig their well," searching for "God's water."

As Christian Salenson points out in his introduction to the volume in which the text of the retreat is published, the Visitation was an important narrative and biblical theme both for Charles de

---

From Christian de Chergé, *Retraite sur le Cantique des cantiques*, ed. Christian Salenson (Bruyères-le-Châtel, France: Éditions Nouvelle Cité, 2013), 74–76.

Foucauld and Louis Massignon before Christian de Chergé. However, it is informative to notice the differences in their respective interpretations. For example, for Foucauld, in his early reflections, the Visitation served as a nonproselytizing model of mission. Mary carries a hidden Jesus, who sanctifies the child in Elizabeth's womb without any need of preaching. Therefore, Foucauld trusts in his own solitary witness to the hidden Jesus as having the potential—without needing to preach—of sanctifying the Touareg Muslims among whom he lives. De Chergé, by way of distinction, emphasizes the mutual interdependency of the children in the wombs of Mary and Elizabeth. Each mother carries a word from God that the other needs to hear and that leaps in its counterpart's presence. De Chergé sees in their meeting an allusion to the dialogue between the Church and Islam generally, and specifically a reflection of his and his friend's Christian–Muslim conversations. Note: The "feast of the virgin" to which Christian de Chergé refers in the opening lines is the feast of the Presentation of the Blessed Virgin Mary, which is celebrated on November 21.

THE MYSTERY OF THE VISITATION

Let's take advantage of this feast of the Virgin by returning to the mystery of the Visitation. It is quite obvious that we should prioritize this mystery of the Visitation in our local Church.

I can easily imagine us in the situation of Mary, going to see her cousin Elizabeth and carrying within herself the same living secret that we too may carry, the living Good News. She received it from an angel. It is her secret, and it is also God's secret. She probably doesn't know how to go about revealing the secret. Should she say something to Elizabeth? Can she? How does she say it? How will it be received? Should it be kept hidden? In the end everything comes spilling out of her, even if she doesn't understand.

It is first of all the secret of God. And something similar happens in Elizabeth's womb. She too is with child. But what Mary doesn't really understand is the bond, the rapport between the child she is carrying and the child Elizabeth is carrying. In fact it would be easier for her to express herself if she understood the connection. But on this precise point, on the mutual dependence between the two children, she has had no revelation. She simply knows that there is a connection, because that is the sign that was given to her: her cousin Elizabeth.

And so it is with our Church, which is each of us, and which carries within itself the Good News. A bit like Mary, first we arrive to be of service (ultimately that was her first intention). But then, carrying this Good News, how should we go about sharing it? And those we have come to meet, we know they are a bit like Elizabeth, bearers of a message that comes from God. Our Church has not told us and does not know exactly what the connection is between the Good News that we carry and this message that gives life to the other. In the end, my Church does not tell me what the bond is between Christ and Islam. So I go to the Muslims without knowing [exactly] what this bond is.

And then, when Mary arrives, it is Elizabeth who speaks first. Well not exactly, since Mary has said: *"As salaam alaikum!"* So that's one thing we can do! We can express peace: "Peace be with you!" And this simple greeting causes something, someone, to stir within Elizabeth. And in the stirring, something was said . . . which was the Good News, not all the Good News, but what could be grasped of it in the moment. "How does this happen to me that . . . the child in me leaped?" [Lk 1:43–44]. Probably it was the child inside

Mary who leaped first. In fact, the whole affair was between the children. . . .

Elizabeth has released the *Magnificat* of Mary. And ultimately, if we are mindful, and if we approach our own encounter with the other in the same way—with attention, a desire to come together, and in need of that which he is and that which he has to say to us—then it is likely he will tell us something that joins with what we carry, showing that we are in accord. . . . It would allow us to expand our Eucharist, because ultimately the *Magnificat* that we are given to sing is the Eucharist. The first Eucharist of the Church was the *Magnificat* of Mary, meaning the need we have of each other to enact the Eucharist: *for you and for the multitude*. . . .

THE WELL

Returning to the image of the well, let's say it's easier when we dig together. I have a very dear friend, a neighbor, who can neither read nor write, and who is surely very busy, even if I don't always notice for lack of attention. One time about fifteen years ago, when he was twenty years old, he asked me to teach him how to pray. It was about teaching him the Muslim way of praying. We have come a long way in that regard. Prayer is a unique path to God. Since then we found ourselves regularly on the same wavelength. But for a while, when I was the guest master, he thought that on weekends I was too busy. He was a neighbor and felt it wasn't right that I couldn't devote a little time to him. So one day he came up with the expression: "You know it's been a long time since we dug our well." It's beautiful . . . and the expression stuck. So from time to time we made an appointment to dig our well. And one day—I told this story at *Journées romaines*—I asked him, a little laughing: "At the bottom of our well, what do you think we will find? Are we going to find Christian water or Muslim water?" But he didn't take it with a laugh [and said]: "We've been together for so long and you are still asking this question? At the bottom of the well, ultimately, we will find God's water." I don't think there is any better response.

Homilies

What is analogously called a "sermon" in many Christian denominations is called a "homily" by Catholics. In the context of mass, an ordained member of the church (deacon, priest, bishop) instructs and inspires the faithful by preaching a message (homily) based on the Bible passages proclaimed that day. Christian de Chergé was ordained a priest in 1964 for the Archdiocese of Paris, and from 1964 to 1969 he served as a chaplain at the Basilica of Sacré Coeur de Montmartre. As Brother André Barbeau's introduction to the volume in which the original texts are published informs us, we do not have any of his homilies from those years, nor from his years at PISAI. The first homily we have is from December 6, 1970, the Second Sunday of Advent, which he preached while still a novice at the Abbey of Notre Dame d'Aiguebelle; the next one is from All Saints' Day, 1975, at Tibhirine. We have a total of 262 published homilies, which were preached on Sundays, the Triduum, and other important feast days. We do not know how closely de Chergé kept to the written texts, but we presume that he, or someone, read the universal prayers of the faithful that follow some of the homilies,

---

From Christian de Chergé, *L'Autre que nous attendons: Homélies de Père Christian de Chergé (1970–1996)* (Monjoyer, France: Éditions de Bellefontaine, 2006).

so we included those prayers here. The titles that accompany the homilies are de Chergé's.

Untitled
December 6, 1970
Second Sunday of Advent, Year C

Texts: Baruch 5:1–9; Philippians 1:4–6, 8–11; Luke 3:4–6

What follows is part of the earliest of Christian de Chergé's published homilies. It is more a set of lengthy notes than a script. In the section we selected, de Chergé touches on many themes that will characterize his spirituality going forward: the discovery of Christ in all people and all people in Christ, the Brother as sacrament, Christian salvation as incomplete without the friendship of non-Christians, an emphasis on living the Gospel joyfully, and understanding salvation as integrated with our lives here and now, rather than as a remote and isolated reality for which we long. Stylistically, he was already capitalizing key words and phrases for emphasis. His several mentions of the Pope refer to Pope Paul VI's November–December 1970 apostolic pilgrimage to several countries in West Asia, Oceania, and Australia.

". . . and all flesh (not: every man)
will see the salvation of God" [Lk 3:6]

. . .

Living the Gospel

How to respond with some clarity to the question posed to us by our contemporaries, "What sort of salvation?" The ambiguity arises from the errors that we Christians have made in our presentation of salvation. Our three texts today, like the example of the Pope, invite us to move beyond [three] views that are too narrow: a salvation "to come," an "eliminatory" salvation, an "individualistic" salvation.

[First], a salvation "to come": for a better world, leading to the condemnation of this world as if God had not created it. We behave as if Christ had not been born, as if His name were not JESUS = Savior, as if even today salvation is not present in this house [Lk 19:9]. The Word [*Verbe*] became flesh so that all flesh may SEE Him during His earthly journey. The salvation of humanity presumes man's dignity, ensuring for ALL the free play of their dynamisms in justice and peace. That is the message of Baruch, who invites us to make this Advent a rediscovery of what God has given us and a sharing of those blessings. Reconciling man with himself. Welcoming our gifts and abilities and using them to serve.

[Second], an "eliminatory" salvation: a number of trials for a salvation presented as arduous, difficult. We have rejected what Christ tells us, skilled at shutting the doors of heaven as if they could only be opened by us. Let us not reduce to prohibitions a salvation that is rooted in possibility; let us not erect barriers where God makes an opening. "In those days, I will pour out my Spirit upon all flesh" [Acts 2:17]. Rather, let us welcome the initiative of God with joy, LOVING it, and articulating our response according to that love. See [Pope] Paul VI's message to Christians: "Discern what is most important" [Phil 1:10]. In prayer, let us be carried by our hearts, making of this ADVENT a time for a free and responsible response to the CALL of God, recognizing a trace of the Spirit in everything that liberates man for greater love. Reconciling man with God. Welcoming with love the ways in which we are called. Paul VI to young

Catholics: "Are you aware that one can only be truly free to the extent that one is responsible?" ["Address to the University World of the Philippines," Manila, November 28, 1970].

[Third], an "individualistic" salvation: in order to reconcile the non-Christian with God, we must first reconcile ourselves with our brother. Yet salvation too often appears as a private affair. If salvation = love, how can one claim to be saved without, or even against, all those whom Jesus Christ calls us to love when we attach ourselves to him? Our brother is in Jesus Christ, the sacrament of our love for God. Paul VI to the young people of Sydney: "You must choose either for man with Jesus Christ, or against man." ["Homily," Sydney, Australia, December 2, 1970]. Reconciling man with man.

Christian salvation is expected in the form of a transformation of the relationships among people. Such indeed is the Word [*Parole*] received by John the Baptist within a heart of prayer, in the desert. In having carried it, in having gone out to others so that they would know how to see, he was the first to recognize this salvation in Jesus Christ: "Behold, the Lamb of God!" [Jn 1:29]. Conversion is truly the introduction of love in place of sin in the relationships between people, and this cannot happen without Jesus Christ (Sydney).

Hence, ADVENT: Awaiting from Jesus Christ an abundance of charity. Through the power that You have bestowed upon Him over ALL FLESH, he grants ETERNAL LIFE. . . . From the depths of the desert, the Word [*Parole*] judges our relationships with our brothers in solitude. Let us come to the desert to learn how to love. Let us treat all men as brothers who await Jesus Christ, and then we will be able to recognize in their faces the trace of his approach. That will be CHRISTMAS. Let us welcome every person as Christ in order to recognize Christ in every person.

Trinity
June 17, 1984
Holy Trinity Sunday, Year A

Texts: Exodus 34:4–9; 2 Corinthians 13:11–13; John 3:16–18

Christian de Chergé's devotion and spirituality were deeply Trinitarian. In the following homily on the Feast of the Holy Trinity, de Chergé frames the "difficult" Christian vocational responsibility for interreligious openness as a participation in the relations of the three persons of God. Perhaps to the frustration of the theologians among his congregants—or among the readers of this collection—de Chergé shows little interest in or patience for systematic Trinitarian difficulties and questions. Instead, his orientation is pastoral, inviting Christians to recognize religious difference as an opportunity for assenting with brothers and sisters (qua Christ) to the oneness of God through the unifying and loving action of the Spirit. Typical is de Chergé's resistance to critics who describe his trust in unity as naïve or passé.

Note: His comment that "He is One, and there is no other but Him" is a reference to the first part of the Muslim profession of faith (shahâda): *There is no god but God* (La ilaha illallah). *We do not know whether de Chergé read aloud the quotation from Elizabeth of the Trinity (1880–1906), which he included in the written text.*

Entry: Formula of the second reading. Recover the baptismal grace that has CO-SIGNED us "in the Name of the Father, and of the Son, and of the Holy Spirit" and the living water that whispers the filial call, "Come to the Father." Enter this celebration of the Trinity as into the very movement of Love, which is the Trinitarian communion open to infinity.

The Trinity? How to explain it? Faith falters, the mind goes astray, and yet we must account for it *hic et nunc*, with the sense, sometimes confused, sometimes intense, that this is where everything converges, or, on the contrary, that this is where everything DIFFERS. Yes, this is certainly where the other's faith provokes us to be coherent and accurate. To express the Trinity, we will posit THREE . . . and our dialogue partner will answer ONE.

However, we must be just as attached to the ONE as the other is. Indeed the presence of the other who is different but also a champion of unity returns us to the shore of communion where TOGETHER we can say that He is ONE, and there is no other but HIM . . . and if a Jewish brother joins us, behold, we will be THREE saying that He is ONE, proclaiming that He is HOLY, even thrice HOLY . . . God, tender and merciful, slow to anger, full of love and fidelity, *rahman, rahim, karim*, from the Exodus to the Hegira, passing through the *Pascha*, a single movement of adoration toward the God three times holy . . . and three times sanctified!

One could say "That's too easy. . . . You've brazenly erased the differences. Gone are the days when we only looked for similarities, with all the risks of syncretism. Today we must have the courage of DIFFERENCE, leaning into it the better to respect the other in his refusal to accept what distinguishes us from him. Leaning into difference the better to respect what makes us unique."

So we can set up camp in our differences, each in his own place, while agreeing to share everything else—the spirit of the times, the beauty of the environment, the joy of life, the urgency to work for creation, and also the hardships of the journey—all that makes us human and nothing more. . . . And then, when the time comes, we will return to our own tents in the intimacy of our own people, with our own God. It's the pattern of the human family, that moment when everyone retreats to their own place. . . . We even left our fathers and mothers to experience this intimacy, of the home, of religious consecration, of prayer.

But even under the tent of the Church the Christian continues to feel torn. . . . Having left everything, he must displace himself yet again, like Christ, in order to be propelled toward the other, sent, in the very name of what differentiates him. A God of Love who wills not that the world be condemned but that it be SAVED, a FATHER to whom we, like the Son, can pray only by affirming that he is OURS, for ALL of us, and with whose Son we can be brothers only by wholeheartedly giving ourselves in opposition to any division or sectarianism. A SPIRIT poured out on every creature whose desire is to UNITE, a SPIRIT who sees no contradiction between the Father and the Son, even though He is the unique and perfect witness of their difference.

Difference exists in God's self, in the absolute of the Persons, for the Father is not the Son . . . but at the same time the difference is relative, for it is effaced by the mutual gift of the Spirit, a Spirit who also sees no contradiction between the Old and New Testaments, since he worked on both and continuously uncovers them as present within each of us. Isn't it He who allows us to sing the Psalms in concert with each other?

Thus the Christian can never settle comfortably into difference, setting up his tent on the mountain of separation. His temple is open. His tent is exposed to the wind. His distinctiveness commits him to the multitude. Here he is, moving toward the other, toward all others, in the very name of the mystery of God who is a COMMUNION of persons. . . . He is also moving toward that ineffable mystery in the name of what the other has to say simply by existing and by being made unique by the grace of the Unique. "Show me a heart that loves," said Saint Augustine, "and it will understand . . . what Trinity means."

How else can we bear witness to this God who is a relationship of love except by entering wholeheartedly into that relationship, open to all? Paul invites us to translate into our lives the unique relationship between the Father and the Son into which we were baptized, responding to the Christian call to embody the Trinitarian life in the world. So that the world may see at work the mystery of love that creates Man in the image and likeness of a GOD who is OPEN, not impersonal, but interpersonal.

Echoing the example of Jesus praising and blessing the Father when a child freely approaches Him, when a woman becomes a sign of tenderness and welcome, when a thief begs for His grace in the name of another kind of justice, each gesture, freely made, is a living sign of the reality that we celebrate today and that resonates throughout the world. LIFE thus takes on the meaning of gift and forgiveness, joy, celebration, sharing, but hunger as well, and of a table open to all, of an infinite light that causes us to proclaim: "This one is like me, bone of my bones, flesh of my flesh, and I need him to exist in fullness" [see Gn 2:23]. That is to follow the example of the Father who finds his delight, that is to say his very Being, his spirit, only in the Son.

Difficult vocation the Christian faith, where one is repeatedly called to go beyond oneself in opening to the other. That is to say, there is a constant adjustment in terms of words and actions . . . and it doesn't matter if we don't know how to articulate the Trinity. . . . Love can't be demonstrated by a proof; to explain it is to betray it! The only way to believe in Love, who is the living God, is to let Love enable us to love fully. That is how the THREE who are but ONE continue to give themselves together to the multitude, forgiving the sin of division, and building communion through our humble gifts, each act of goodwill, a simple glass of water, the bread and wine of this filial offering.

Note: Elizabeth of the Trinity, "The capacity of the soul, expanded at the Master's arrival, seems to leave itself to traverse the walls of the immensity of the One who arrives, and this phenomenon occurs: It is God who, in our depths, receives God coming to us, and God contemplates God! God, in whom all beatitude resides!"

Prayers:

- Make our Church a people that belong to You in justice and fidelity . . .
- Send upon all believers the Spirit Who will unite us in the very love the Son has for You . . .
- Allow all peoples to forge new paths of peace, sharing, understanding, and cooperation . . .
- That each of us may leave this Eucharistic celebration strengthened, connected to all by the unique name You bestow upon him through Your Son . . .

CONVERSION and Cross, Christ
April 17, 1987—Good Friday, Year A

Texts: Isaiah 52:13–53:12; Hebrews 4:14–16; 5:7–9; John 18[19]:1–19, 42

While Christian de Chergé rarely preached on Easter Sunday, he often preached during the Triduum, and we have included several of those homilies here. The cross is a major focus of de Chergé's spirituality and theology, but as we see in his later chapter talks, he is concerned not to isolate either the event or the meaning of the cross from the rest of Jesus's life and from the Incarnation. In this homily, he brings forth the paradox of the cross as the site of aversion and conversion, succinctly captured in his last lines. We also glimpse here his occasional style of bringing the hearer into an impressionistic gathering of scriptural passages and images.

"Everything is accomplished . . ." [Jn 19:28]. And is it a failure? Conversion reaching its human terminus. We remember his first words: "Be converted!" [see Mk 1:15].

A conversion in action: an entire life given to God and to men. The conversion of a humanity which is that of the Word [*Verbe*] of God. No distance in Him between Word [*Parole*] and actions. The cry "I THIRST!" [Jn 19:28] involves the entire movement of his being. Everything he lived takes on the meaning of this fundamental orientation of the Word [*Verbe*], whose nature is to be TURNED toward the Father.

In this moment of "accomplishment," we find everything that prevents us, blocks us, everything that provokes in us AVERSION instead of CONVERSION.

Physical suffering, no doubt: giving birth.

Hatred, jealousy, betrayal of friends: "Take courage, I have CONQUERED!" [Jn 16:33].

The Law: conversion means going beyond. FREEDOM. "According to our law, he ought to die" [Jn 19:7].

Obedience: submission to a stronger authority. That of our own heart united to the Heart of God. "You would have no power!" [Jn 19:11].

The CROSS . . . the unique symbol of all that we refuse, and henceforth the site of a GAP. To this we must convert if we want to give our life its greatest scope—height, depth, length, width—and its true trajectory: ascension. The site, the hour, the mode of the great REFUSAL converted into the site, hour, and mode of the greatest LEAP forward toward the ultimate reality, beyond the appearances of the moment (from which we turn away).

Behold the MAN! [Jn 19:5].
Behold your KING! [Jn 19:14].
Behold your MOTHER! [Jn 19:27].

Behold the CRUCIFIED ONE.... Isaiah was right to prophesy him: he is indeed like the one from whom we turn away, and yet, conversion was also announced, it is THERE: "They will look upon the one they have pierced!" [Zech 12:10; Isa 53:5]. A convergence of gazes. A sign of conversion open to all, for a COMMUNION in LOVE.

Yes, the CROSS is a sign of horror and provokes aversion. "Do not do to others as you have done to me."

Yes, the CROSS is a sign of an unimaginable love that provokes conversion. "Do to others as I have done for you!"

Called to Humility
March 24, 1989—Good Friday, Year C

Texts: Isaiah 52:13–53:12; Hebrews 4:14–16; 5:7–9; John 18:1–19, 42

In this homily, we see several typical features of Christian de Chergé's spirituality and theology: a Trinitarian reading of the crucifixion, Jesus as the embodiment of humility, and Mary as the model witness for Christians. Also, even more than in his 1986 Good Friday homily, here de Chergé exposes the cross and our complicity in it as ongoing realities.

Notes: "Called to Humility" was the theme of the upcoming Ribât Catholic–Muslim dialogue. "Satanic verse" refers to a controversial and disputed tradition within Islamic history that alleges that the Prophet Muhammad was influenced by Satan to include polytheistic verses into the Qur'an, which he subsequently removed. Adapting the story for a Christian context, de Chergé suggests that we who, in our pride, call for the crucifixion of Christ, historically and today, have been influenced by Satan. Rather than use different words, we translated both orgueil *and* fierté *as* pride *to preserve de Chergé's direct contrast of the two terms in the final lines of the homily.*

This is the place, this is the time for us to be challenged by this theme (upcoming *Ribât*).

Yet, humility seems dead. We crucified it; we placed a cross upon it. Its whole way of being weighed upon us, judged us. It was so humiliating to feel it at our side, so incomprehensibly humble and gentle of heart. He had EVERYTHING he needed to succeed . . . everything we dream of. Some of us would say we were right to punish him. It was all hiding an immeasurable pride [*orgueil*]: claiming to have God for his Father!

And so we arrive at an impasse! Everything that constitutes our pride [*orgueil*] is there too, pitiful and naked, disfigured, ridiculed by us, crucified with Him. That mocking crown, the royal title, the elevated throne, the body stripped, emptied. The full extent of the Law applied, hardening us in our hatred and solitude. The Feast of Passover inaugurated in blood that has already lost its life. And we who believed in Him, we are left with this shame, this stain that confronts us again today: a crucified Messiah. Scandal, folly. We'd like to turn the page, quickly, and, who knows, even pick ourselves up in the pride [*fierté*] of having been right. He resurrected others!

And yet our humiliation remains. We have no reason to boast, "If we had been there!" We are no better than those who at that time shouted: "DEATH! DEATH!" The only true

"Satanic verse" of Scripture, if it is written, is due to our having uttered it. And it remains WRITTEN, forever. God used us to reveal us to ourselves. We find it so easy to take down the other: his behavior embarrasses us, his humility humiliates us. "Let's crucify him!"

But no, humility is not dead. It has already risen, there, standing *at the foot of the Cross*, infinitely worthy. MARY! *His mother . . . and also the disciple he loved, and the other Mary.* A river descends, a life rises. The dry tree will turn green again.

And we are seized with vertigo. Humility is not what we believed. Nor life. Nor man. Let us try it on for ourselves. For us, it is a clown's costume. For him, it is the "seamless tunic, woven in one piece, from the top down" [Jn 19:23], from ABOVE! The one who comes from ABOVE knows this secret of God like all the others.

The secret/vertigo of the WORD [*Verbe*] that never ceases to incarnate himself in the least things, until the very end: a few drops of vinegar when he says: "I THIRST" [Jn 19:28].

The vertigo of the SPIRIT who must communicate life through death: "He handed over his Spirit!" [Jn 19:30].

The secret/vertigo of the Father himself who accepted everything without saying a word. We have humiliated God in the extreme. It is we who cried out just now: "We have no KING but Caesar!" [Jn 19:15]. And God kept silent. He allowed it to happen.

The secret/vertigo of MAN called to something greater than himself. A calling that no pride [*orgueil*] can imagine! *ECCE HOMO!* "Behold the MAN!" [Jn 19:5]. *Humus, human, humility*: our poor words bespeak our common origin and our common destiny.

Thus our eyes were lifted. They no longer dared to look him in the face. Now something attracts us, a PRIDE [*fierté*] greater than all pride [*orgueil*], our ultimate dimension and our true place, in the open Heart. The humility of God, our own, is there to be CONTEMPLATED.

Pride [*orgueil*] may be from the heart, but it's a heart CLOSED in on itself. Humility is the open heart of God that becomes contagious by giving itself to be contemplated. May ours open and enter into a religion of humility.

The "Martyrdom" of Love [*charité*]
March 31, 1994 — Holy Thursday, Year B

Texts: Exodus 12:1–8, 11–14; 1 Corinthians 11:23–26; John 13:1–15

Along with his final Testament, *the following homily is among the best examples of Christian de Chergé's mature spirituality. The monks' brush with mortal danger, on Christmas Eve 1993, had occurred three months earlier. De Chergé now encourages his brothers to persevere in their monastic vocation by turning to the life and mission of Jesus as their model. This is the first in an extraordinary series of homilies dedicated to various "martyrdoms," namely, of love, innocence, hope, and the Holy Spirit, all included in this collection. From various angles, de Chergé unwinds the commonsense notion of martyrdom as a glorious death and, instead, recovers the original sense of martyrdom as* witness. *Jesus washing his disciples' feet, rather than his crucifixion, becomes the primary image for meditating on his martyrdom, and the monks' "martyrdom" likewise commits them to repeated, mundane, humble acts of loving service toward both friends and enemies. De Chergé's triple use of "from experience" in the last paragraphs demonstrates for his brothers that in fact they already have been living a martyrdom of love.*

Notes: *In this homily and throughout the collection, we have translated both* charité *and* amour *as* love, *but we have indicated the few places de Chergé used* charité *by retaining the French term in brackets. That is, if not otherwise indicated,* love = amour. *While it seems he is employing the terms interchangeably, perhaps readers will discover another pattern in his usage. We always translate* martyre *as* martyrdom. *We usually translate* martyr *as* martyr *and* témoignage *as* witness. *However, for the sake of consistency in meaning and to avoid verbal redundancy, we sometimes translate* martyr *as* witness *and* témoignage *as* testimony. *"Acts" refer to a genre of Christian literature called* Acta Martyrum, *accounts of the suffering and death of Christians in various contexts of persecution. Notre Dame d'Afrique is the basilica in Algiers, a site of pilgrimage and host to many important ceremonial events. An inscription behind the altar reads: "Our Lady of Africa, pray for us and for the Muslims." Bernardo Olivera, OCSO (b. 1943), was abbot general of the Cistercians of the Strict Observance from 1990 to 2008, so he was in regular contact with the monks of Tibhirine during their final years. In the opening pages of his early reflections on the deaths of the monks* (How Far to Follow?) *he graciously concedes Christian's point about the connection between monks and martyrs. The "Bosnian Muslim" de Chergé mentions refers to a survivor of the December 14, 1993, massacre at Tamesguida. When confronted by the attackers, this man declared that he was a Muslim, recited the* shahâda *as proof (Islamic testimony of faith), and vouched that several of his co-workers were also Muslim, thereby saving all of their lives. Marie-Christine Ray has since suggested that the "Bosnian Muslim" and his co-workers were actually Christians, which would in no way diminish his heroism (Ray,* Christian de Chergé, *190–91)."*

The washing of feet, the shared cup and bread, the cross . . . one single commandment of love, one single WITNESS. It is the witness of Jesus, his *testamentum*, in Greek μαρτύριον [*marturion*] the "martyrdom" of Jesus.

There are many "martyrs" presently in our country. In one camp as in the other, each honors its dead under the glorious title of "martyrs," in Arabic *shouhada* (plural of *shahîd*), from the same root as *shahâda*, the Muslim profession of faith.

We ourselves have long understood "martyr" in the unique sense of a relationship with faith, of a testimony given at the same time to Christ and to Christian dogma. Some "Acts" of martyrs surprise us by the assuredness of their faith.

We live in a time when faith does not exclude doubt or questioning. There is often in these "Acts" something that throws us off-balance and stuns us today: the hardness of these witnesses of the faith vis-à-vis their judges, their self-understanding as being "pure," the certitude expressed that their persecutor will go straight to hell. A fundamentalism already, or at least one could be tempted to think so.

Here, at the hour of his passage in faith toward the Father, Jesus indeed "purifies," but through love. The one who is not "pure," he still calls "Friend!"

It took until the end of the twentieth century for the Church to recognize as martyrdom a testimony less of faith than of supreme love [*charité*]: Maximilian Kolbe, martyr of love [*charité*]. . . . And yet it is written, and we have just heard it again: "Having loved his own, he loved them to the end, to the extreme . . ." [Jn 13:1], the extreme of himself, the extreme of the other, the extreme of humanity, of every human being, even of that man who, just now, will go out into the night after having received the morsel of bread, his feet still damp from having been washed.

A few verses after our story, John recalls Psalm 40: "The

friend, in whom I trusted, and who shared my bread, has lifted his heel against me" [Ps 41:9]. The heel that has just been washed, here it is rising. Love has bathed the feet of the future missionaries, and also, in the same spirit, those feet that will now make a backwards journey, one of betrayal, of complicity in murder.

The witness of Jesus until death, his "martyrdom," is a martyrdom of love, of love for humanity, for every human being, even for thieves, even for assassins and executioners, those who act in the darkness, ready to treat you like a "butcher's animal" (Ps 49), or to torture you to death, because one of yours has become one of "theirs." However, he had admonished: "If you love only your friends, what are you doing that is exceptional? Even the pagans (the *kouffâr*) do the same!" [Mt 5:47]. For him, friends and enemies are to be received from the same Father: "You are all brothers!" [Mt 23:8].

That's because a martyrdom of love includes forgiveness. It is the perfect gift, the one that God gives without reserve. So that washing feet, sharing bread, offering his death and forgiving, it's all one and it's for everyone: *For you, and for the multitude, for the remission of sins.* It's the place of the greatest freedom, because that is where the choice of the Son coincides completely with the Father's choice of love. So yes, he can say: "My life, no one takes it, but I give it freely!" [Jn 10:18]. It is given once and for all, for Judas as for Peter, for the two thieves at his sides as for Mary Magdalene and John at the foot of the cross, as for his own mother. This is his final word, his "ultimate teaching," "to make the love of man the test, the criterion, the touchstone of the love of God" (Maurice Zundel).

To give one's life for the love of God, in advance, without condition, is what we [monks] have done . . . or at least what we believed we were doing. We did not ask why or how. We entrusted to God the use of this gift, its expression day after day, until the end.

Alas! We have all lived enough to know that it is impossible for us to do everything out of love, and therefore to claim that our life is a witness of love, a "martyrdom" of love. "Genius is to love," writes Jean d'Ormesson, "and Christianity is ingenious." That's right, but it's not me!

From experience, we know that small gestures often cost a lot, especially when they have to be repeated every day. Washing the feet of one's brothers on Holy Thursday, sure, but if it had to be done daily? When Fr. Bernardo tells us that the Order needs monks more than "martyrs," he is evidently not talking about the martyrdom that a monk undertakes through so many little things. We have given our hearts "wholesale" to God, and it costs us dearly for Him to take it from us piece by piece. Putting on an apron, like Jesus, can be just as significant and solemn as giving one's life . . . and vice versa, giving one's life can be just as simple as putting on an apron. We must remind ourselves of this when the daily gestures or displacements of love become heavy with the threat that we share with others.

From experience, we know that it is easier to give to this person than to that person, to love this brother or sister rather than that one, even in community. Yet the professional conscience of a doctor, the oath he has taken, leads him to care for all his patients, "even the devil," as Brother Luc would add. And doesn't our professional oath, as religious (but already at our baptism!), compel us to love everyone, "even the devil," if God asks us to do so? What should we be doing? That's what we were trying to convey by refusing to take sides; not to retreat into a neutrality that washes its hands—which is impossible—but to remain free to love everyone, because that is our choice, in the name of Jesus and with His grace. If I have given my life to all Algerians, then I have also given it to the "emir" S. A. [Sayah Attiyah]. He will not take it from me, even if he decides to inflict upon me the same treatment suffered by our Croatian friends. At the same time I fervently desire that he will respect my life in the name of the love that God has also inscribed in his vocation as a man. Jesus could not desire the betrayal of Judas. Still calling him "friend," he addresses himself to the love buried within him. He seeks his Father in this man. I even believe that he met him again.

From experience, we know that this martyrdom of love [*charité*] is not exclusive to Christians. We can receive this testimony from anyone as a gift of the Spirit. Behind all the victims that the Algerian tragedy has already counted, who can know how many authentic "martyrs" of a simple and free love there are? We can think of that man who the other day saved the life of an injured policeman near Notre-Dame d'Afrique. A few days later, he paid for this gesture with his own life. And the Bosnian Muslim who saved his fellow workers, he too risked his life. From further back in time, I cannot forget Mohamed, who, one day, protected my life by risking his own . . . and who was murdered by his brothers because he refused to hand his friends over to them. He did not want to have to choose between one and the other. *Ubi caritas . . . Deus ibi est!*

Thus we are brought back to the witness of Jesus, to His martyrdom: "There is no greater love than to give one's life for one's friends. . . . You are all my friends!" [Jn 15:13–15]. We receive this witness with the awareness that "the spirit is willing, but the flesh is weak" [Mt 26:41]. That is precisely why he leaves us his flesh to eat, to assimilate, as the Bread of our witness. . . .

The "Martyrdom" of Innocence
April 1, 1994—Good Friday, Year B

Texts: Isaiah 52:13–53:12; Hebrews 4:14–16, 5:7–9; John 18:1–19, 42

"He was not slaughtered. No, God did not let the beast slit his turtledove's throat" (Ps 73) [74:19]. He was certainly tortured, and his slow death on the cross was a harsh agony . . . but is it necessary to evoke here the other refinements of cruelty that the human beast has invented against his fellow man before and since Calvary, still today, and so close to us? Must we put into perspective the sufferings of Christ, which nonetheless say something essential to our faith?

If they speak so strongly to us, it is undoubtedly because we decipher in them a witness, a "martyrdom" of which we are in need. Yesterday we spoke of the "martyrdom of love" [*charité*]. Couldn't love have been expressed just as well or better without leaving behind the joys of Paradise? Man's rejection of love has caused him to suffer violence. In the Passion of Jesus, we must recognize, as Brother Christophe invited us on Sunday, the witness, the "martyrdom" of nonviolence: the "revenge" of a God whose hands are empty, even nailed.

Only he is truly nonviolent who has been violent neither toward heaven nor earth. Today we are invited to celebrate, before this corpse of a humanity violated by violent men, another kind of testimony, which we all need if we are to escape the insidious complicity that violence finds in each of us. [We need] the witness, the martyrdom of INNOCENCE.

Naturally I am reminded of what Gilles [Nicolas] observed when we gathered here to unite the sacrifice of the Croatians with that of Jesus (December 16): "This year the massacre of the Innocents preceded Christmas!" As a result, we confess the innocence of those little children massacred because one of them represented an anonymous threat to the ruling power. At the same time, we confess the innocence of that Child, born in the night of Bethlehem, whom we now find in the darkness of Golgotha.

Let us not pretend, however, that our Croatian brothers were choirboys. No more than we are! The innocence that we recognize in them all the same is directly linked to the torment they suffered. No, they did not deserve that! It took a disproportionately violent and inhumane retribution to help us rediscover in them the mark of innocence and to proclaim it as the foundation of every man's right to respect for his life.

Rejecting the death penalty, even for criminals, not wishing death for the guilty, is to confess this conviction. *A fortiori* we are all wounded and bruised when blindness and hatred invent tortures in order to seek vengeance, or simply for the pleasure of watching the blood flow. Thus . . . a man joined the resistance; someone went to his house looking for his two younger brothers—twenty-two and seventeen years old. A few days later, the father was summoned by the police, who returned two dead bodies to him, horribly mutilated, without any explanation other than the order of silence. And there are so many examples like this! So much horror leaves us speechless. We almost reproach ourselves for still being alive. What did they do to deserve this? What have we done to still be here, more or less unharmed? We are told: "You are not foreigners like the others, you monks!" Cold comfort. For us solidarity speaks louder than the mere right to life. It is impossible to wash our hands with Pilate: "It's their business. I am INNOCENT of this man's blood!" "Not responsible" [Mt 27:24]. Who can say that? I understand Janine Chanteur when she reproaches Job for proclaiming his innocence: "By pleading not guilty with such stubbornness, don't you see, Job, you are being even more inhuman . . . ? We have done nothing wrong, and yet it is our fault!" (*Les petits enfants de Job*).

The very word "innocent" says it all. It expresses, within our language, the rupture of sin. In the Hellenistic world at least, a negative theology had to be invented to speak of God without too many more-or-less idolatrous anthropomorphisms. Likewise, we have needed the words of a negative anthropology to get back to the core of man, beyond the corrupted nature which is only a shadow of its original opposite: not guilty, nonviolent, innocent, that is to say, harm-less, not capable of causing harm. But who is innocent? We recognize ourselves in the cry of this mother (Janine Chanteur again), confronted like so many others with the "innocent misfortune" of her disabled child: "How can one be innocent when the victim has done nothing wrong?"

So here we are, facing the "victim who has done nothing wrong," to welcome his witness, his martyrdom, and to discover the unique and gripping density of this martyrdom, that of innocence. *Love Alone Is Credible* is the title of a beautiful book by [Hans] Urs von Balthasar. Perhaps even more profoundly, only innocence is credible. This supreme dignity was revealed before our eyes, on the cross. To confess it, we only need to know that we do not possess it. But am I really convinced that I am an accomplice to *that*? Poor mixed-up men that we are, before the Cross, we plead not guilty, like Pilate! Will we leave him alone to be "counted among the wicked"? [Lk 22:37]. I recognize myself well in the paradox that my friend Mohamed expressed in prayer this very morning: "God, hear us. Excuse us! Forgive us. We have done nothing wrong!"

Homilies | 85

At Calvary, it is a criminal who opens my eyes: "This man has done nothing wrong! For us, it is justice!" [Lk 23:41]. And Judas remains an apostle when he testifies: "I have sinned by delivering innocent blood." Those who reply to him, "What does it matter to us? It's your affair!," bear the heavier sin [Mt 27:4].

In front of the innocent one, we cannot remain satisfied with the reflex of claiming only one's own faults, as in the Qur'anic verse: "To me my deeds, and to you yours! You declare yourself innocent of what I do. I declare myself innocent of what you do" (Q 10:41). Job defended himself every step of the way: "Until I die I will maintain my innocence" (Job 27:5). He will have to undergo a journey of conversion that leads to silence, finally putting his mouth in the dust, like the prophet Elijah: "Take my life, for I am no better than my elders" [1 Kgs 19:4].

Yes, only that one could have said: "I have committed no fault, neither sin nor evil, Lord!" (Ps 58) [Ps 59:4–6]. And yet, he never proclaimed himself "innocent." He did not wash his hands. Saint Paul even says: "He became SIN for us!" [2 Cor 5:21]. He only posed the question: "Which one of you convicts me of sin?" [see Jn 8:46]. Innocence does not accuse. Then, when everything was settled for him by our injustice and cowardice, he pleaded "not guilty" for us: "Father, forgive them, for they do not know what they are doing!" [Lk 23:34]. The Innocence that forgives everything.

It is then that the heavens tear apart: the innocence of man and that of God can burst forth together: "It is in this innocence, in this eternal childhood that the Mystery of God, which reveals itself in Jesus Christ, lies," Maurice Zundel said in tonight's reading. "And this God, this God who is free in himself, this God who never looks at himself, this God who does not delight solely in himself, this God who only exists in giving himself (this God who is therefore completely opposite to what sin has done to me), of what world can this God be the Creator if not of a world that is free, free even in the last fibers of its existence?"

Indeed, the creation of the world can now reclaim its place in the divine innocence that is its original matrix. In Arabic, the root of *innocent* (*BaRîoun*) means to CREATE; in Hebrew, *to bring forth from nothingness*. Then, in a second sense, it means *to heal, to free from evil, to absolve*. It testifies that lost innocence can be recovered; it has not been completely destroyed. It still exists somewhere, at the core of each one of us. Jesus testifies to this for us: "Ecce homo!" It is Pilate who says it "innocently," thus designating our first and last innocence, of which here is the "martyr," the witness. At the foot of the Cross, this innocence is present, as if waiting for herself. She has a name and a face: MARY, the new Eve. She is ready to give birth to us anew, ALL of us: "Behold your mother!" [Jn 19:27]. "Dwelling place of my glory, full of grace . . ." [Jn 1:14].

The "Martyrdom" of Hope
April 2–3, 1994 — Easter Vigil, Year B

Texts: Genesis 1:1–2:2; 22:1–18;
Exodus 14:15–15:1; Isaiah 54:5–14;
55:1–11; Baruch 3:9–4:4; Ezekiel 36:16–28;
Romans 6:3–11; Mark 16:1–8

Although it is not made explicit in what follows, readers who are familiar with the theologian and poet Charles Peguy (1873–1914) will notice his influence on Christian de Chergé's treatment of hope.

Notes: Except where indicated, the word translated as silence *is* mutisme, *whose plain sense indicates a lack, or loss, of the ability to speak. Except where indicated, every mention of* hope *translates* espérance. *When de Chergé directly compares* espérance *with* espoir—*both of which can be expressed as* hope *in English—we translate the latter as* hopefulness. *We could have translated it as* optimism, *but in addition to capturing his contrast between the divine and human origins of the virtues, we wanted to preserve the root shared by both terms. Except where indicated, the term* word *translates* parole. *Near the end of the homily, when de Chergé contrasts the human and divine origins of words, as* mot *and* Verbe *respectively, we retain the original in brackets. While not his universal practice, in this homily de Chergé capitalizes the pronouns that refer to Jesus, so we have as well. Finally, sometimes de Chergé retains second-person pronouns even after he exits the Gospel narrative for which the "you" was germane, so we have as well.*

> "They said nothing to anyone,
> for they were afraid" [Mk 16:8]

Silence and fear! And we sang "Alleluia!" We illuminated everything; we offered peace to one another; now these last two notes at the conclusion of our long celebration of the Word; what strange *Good News*! Silence and fear.... It sounds so out of place that the "pastoral" advice is generally given to stop reading the text two verses earlier: "There you will see him!" [Mk 16:7].

It's impossible for us to stop before the end of this Gospel Word, given our reality for these many months.

Our entire environment participates in a tangible atmosphere of silence and fear that poisons the country and paralyzes it. And within us, how often we share those same reactions as events, information, and encounters unfold. We are not proud of it. None of us, I believe, has escaped it . . . except perhaps our brother Luc. A friend shares the rule he set for himself: "Be silent and hide!" (True, he is a hermit!).

Indeed, all these forms of witness, of "martyrdom," that we have been talking about these past few days, are they not often tainted, stopped in their tracks by these two instinctual brakes: silence and fear? They weigh heavily on the witness of faith, on that of nonviolence, on what we called the "martyrdom" of love [*charité*] or that of innocence. We readily identified ourselves with Peter, denying, and with Pilate, letting things unfold.

Silence and fear, here the Gospel grants them their rights of citizenship. Better than that, according to the strongest testimonies, they constitute the last two words of the Gospel of Mark. Could there be a Gospel silence and a Gospel fear that would be capable of evangelizing our own? Perhaps even turning [our own silence and fear] into evangelizers?

Let us retrace the events. First, these women were not lacking in courage, hastening toward the tomb. There they were, the first to rise for a job that would have required some men as well, because there was that stone to be rolled away. But the men were not there. It's amazing how, around this body they have come to embalm, everything seems to be beginning: the day—it's early morning; the week—it's the first day; the sun—it's just rising; the perfumes—they've just come from the shop; it's at first glance that they see the stone rolled away; they are still on the threshold. . . . And then everything becomes unsettled. It's an absolute beginning. They are beside themselves, caught up in an experience that closely resembles that of the disciples during the Transfiguration. The witness dressed in white has told them: "Do not be afraid!" [Mk 16:6] and "Go and tell . . . !" [Mk 16:7], but they flee, trembling, and instead there is silence and fear. Fear of an absolute beginning that surprised them at the very place where everything seemed to be ending. There is an inchoate sense that this is not just a simple starting over, even if he is "waiting for you in Galilee," as in your first encounters with Him, even if he continues to "go before" so that you can continue to follow Him [Mk 16:7].

It was enough for this outsider witness to stand in the place of the Crucified, for [the women] to enter, with all their hearts, into this *beyond* of the death that will give their faith the dimension of HOPE: "Christ, our hope, dies no more; over Him death has no power!" [Rom 6:9]. They had believed in Him . . . but now, for three days He had been dead. They came to embalm His body. They came to embalm their faith in Him. Since then, many others have succeeded in doing so! But He is no longer there. Their balm is pointless. One does not embalm the "one who goes before." One does not embalm hope that is underway; hope has seized you, and yet it remains ahead, elusive. The one in whom we hope, we no longer see him, even when he is dead. In fact, maybe that's Him, the young man dressed in white? It is He, and He alone, who can carry our HOPE in his orbit, simply because He goes before us, to Galilee, and to the ends of the earth. But now he is no longer in the world, and his witnesses know very well that they are no longer "of this world" [Jn 17:11–16]. They must give an account of the hope that has surpassed death and overcome the world [1 Pet 3:15]. Here they are "thrown out of themselves" toward the unknown that passes through an empty tomb where the space remains unclaimed. One must die to oneself, without a word [*mot*], because words [*mots*] fail when the Word [*Verbe*] is no longer there to offer them.

The silence and fear of the women lie precisely at the intersection of the faith that knows how to speak, even with boldness, and the hope that must accept its own logic of silence [*silence*] and distance. The Holy Spirit will establish the connection.

It seems to me that today we receive an additional call to the "martyrdom" for which we are destined, one of HOPE. Oh! It is neither glorious nor brilliant. It takes the exact shape of all the dimensions of daily life. It has always defined the monastic state: step by step, drop by drop, word by word, elbow to elbow . . . and this must be started again and again in a regimented life, every morning, into every night, and we must continue to meditate, to correct, to discern, above all to wait. This is the path by which "he goes before us," "from beginning to beginning, by beginnings that have no end . . ." to speak like our father Saint Gregory of Nyssa.

And our "Galilee," where we have chosen to follow Him, in this time and place, where He is BEFORE us, is this country of Algeria, in its paschal today. Only hope can keep us here in our place. It took Moussa to remind us, as if by instinct, shortly after the Christmas "visit": "We, like you," he said, "can only get through by hopefulness. If you leave, we will lose your hopefulness, and we will lose ours!" He spoke of hopefulness [*espoir*]. It is up to us to translate it into hope [*espérance*], that is, beyond the horizon blocked by the threat of death, since it is there that "he goes before us." The insecurity of the place and the moment, the condition of being a foreigner, the caution to be observed, is this not the classic currency of the regime of hope? Let us not forget our trust in the other and the journey traveled together, whose truth, it is impossible to deny, persists, even when the encounter becomes rarer and more contentious.

As witnesses of this Easter hope, we are challenged to embody it if we wish to exorcize our too-immediate fears and give them the meaning and value of encounters with the Absolute God. We are also invited there by the beautiful Qur'anic verse that asserts, "Whosoever hopes [*yarajû*] for the meeting with God, God's term is coming" (Q 29:5). In this way, even our fears can contribute to bringing us closer to God:

- Fear of tomorrow, overcome by the patience of each today, for ultimately tomorrow belongs only to God and to the paschal glory . . .
- Fear of violent death, overcome by the presence of the Living One of Easter bearing the stigmata . . .
- Fear of civil war, overcome by the certainty that PEACE is not of this world, no more than the witnesses of the Risen One that we are . . .
- Fear of Islam and of other believers tempted by intolerance, a fear also overcome in advance by the gift of the Spirit creating the communion of saints, so often "a wonder before our eyes . . ."

Therefore, we need this Easter hope that tells us, like the women in the Gospel, that if everything continues, nothing will be as it was before. On this most holy night, let us reaffirm the YES of our baptism to the One who goes before us on earth as in heaven (and now in heaven as on earth); and let us join the cohort of these witnesses whom we declare to be just and holy because they have known how to hope against all hope. It is from within silence and fear, as from within the tomb, that hope can rise, alive like a cry, the cry of the witness, of the "martyr," from age to age: "He is risen, ALLELUIA!"

The Martyrdom of the Holy Spirit
May 22, 1994—Pentecost, Year B

Texts: Acts 2:1–11; Galatians 5:16–25; John 15:26–16:15

This is the last of Christian de Chergé's homilies on martyrdom, and in some ways it is the thematic culmination of the series. De Chergé proclaims that the Holy Spirit—not Jesus, as the mainstream of Catholic tradition would expect—is the "martyr par excellence." He also shares an example of a Muslim who participates in martyrdom, as de Chergé understands it, not only witnessing to love and hope but also participating in the witness of the Holy Spirit.

Notes: Eid al-Adha *is the Islamic commemoration of Abraham's near-sacrifice of his son, which Muslims celebrate with the ritual slaughter of a lamb, goat, or other animal. Those with enough wealth share the meat with those in need.* Eid al-Adha *also marks the conclusion of Hajj, the annual pilgrimage of Muslims to Mecca. It is called the "greater feast"* (Eid al-Kabîr) *in relation to* Eid al-Fitr, *the "lesser feast"* (Eid al-Saghîr), *which marks the conclusion of the Islamic month of fasting, Ramadan. When the GIA began targeting foreigners for assassination, they sought Islamically grounded approval for doing so. Sheikh Mohamed Bouslimani (1936–1993) fought for Algerian independence from France and later openly criticized the FLN, the ruling party of the new country. He was a highly respected jurist among Islamist partisans. When, however, he refused to justify the murder of civilians on religious grounds, or any grounds at all, he was kidnapped and murdered by his opponents. In 1990 John Paul II wrote* Redemptoris Missio, *"On the Permanent Validity of the Church's Missionary Mandate," which nonetheless invites Catholics to observe the work of the Holy Spirit outside the visible bounds of the church.*

Henri Vergès (1930–1994), a Marist Brother, and Paule-Hélène Saint Raymond (1927–1994), a Little Sister of the Assumption, were the first of the nineteen Catholic martyrs of the Algerian civil war. They were murdered on May 8, 1994, two weeks before this homily was preached.

"It is the Spirit who bears witness . . ." (1 Jn 5:6)

Pentecost . . . on the day after *Eid al-Adha*, the "Feast of Sacrifice," the "greater feast" (*Eid al-Kabîr*). Pentecost is also a "great feast"! "So, what do you sacrifice, what do you slaughter?," a young [Muslim] neighbor asked me. I am inclined to answer, "I offer the multitude of WITNESSES who, ever since the event we are celebrating, have never ceased to give their lives for the proclamation of the Gospel, following the example of their Master and Lord."

Indeed, isn't Pentecost first and foremost the great feast of WITNESS, that is, of "martyrdom" (in Greek), of *shahâda* (in Arabic)? The apostles were there, cloistered in their fear, but faithfully waiting in prayer for what Jesus had promised. And then, the doors open. A great rush of wind fills their being. Tongues are untied. Hearts expand to the ends of the world, all of which is gathered there, although the apostles had not yet noticed. Soon Peter will speak: "This Jesus . . . God has raised him. We are witnesses of it" (Acts 2:32). Later he would add the necessary clarification that eluded him in that initial moment, when they were so united to the new power that propelled them to testify: "We are witnesses of these things, we and the HOLY SPIRIT, whom God has given to those who obey him" (Acts 5:32).

Jesus had foretold this to them: "When the Advocate comes, whom I will send to you from the Father, the Spirit of truth who proceeds from the Father, he will WITNESS in my favor. And you also, you will bear witness" (Jn 15:26). This is the Good News, the Gospel of this day. We proclaim that the Holy Spirit has been given, and we testify that he testifies within us. It is the "great feast" of the witness of the Spirit, without which the witness of the Church, the apostles, and our own would be null and in vain. We celebrate the GIFT of this Witness who never ceases to communicate Himself, from generation to generation, from language to language, from life to life, like a relay race, carrying the flame of Love into the depths of hearts.

We celebrate the "martyrdom" of the Holy Spirit. "There is no greater love than to give one's life for those whom one loves" (Jn 15:13). This is the witness of Jesus, his Paschal mystery. It has been, from all eternity, the witness of God. If the Holy Spirit is the "martyr" *par excellence*, it is because He is the living gift that the Father and the Son mutually give of everything they are. He is LIFE in God, eternally given, and now communicated to the world for a new creation involving the blood and suffering of a laborious birth.

It seems that this first "witness" of the Spirit, presiding over the genesis, existed outside of time, in the serenity of a perfect construction. Everything was good. . . . He hovered over the waters of the primordial baptism, in the love of the Father, where the Word [*Verbe*] awakened all things. This "martyrdom" was that of a shared happiness. It was unaware of suffering and spilled blood. It was self-sufficient. It was deeply inscribed, like a seal, an image, a likeness. Even today, it sometimes emerges, a virginal trace of an initial grace in a child's heart that evil may have brushed against but not defiled. . . .

In Jesus, this witness has been resurrected. Man is restored to himself. With all His strength, the Spirit comes to testify that this is what the Father wanted for us. This is what He comes to accomplish in us, with patience toward our chaotic journeys. This witness is there, watching and never despairing. He knows that, in every person, Christ seeks and fulfills Himself.

"The Holy Spirit Himself bears witness that we are children of God" (Rom 8:16). He is the Witness who arouses witnesses; He is the "martyr" without whom there is no martyrdom. He alone can verify the testimony. Jesus's words are clear: "Do not worry! The Holy Spirit will teach you what to say and do . . ." [Lk 12:12]. And this Witness, this *shahîd*, tells us not to be satisfied with purely verbal *shahâda*, "They preach but they do not practice!" [Mt 23:3]. This *shahîd* tells us that the witness is known by his fruits. According to Saint Paul (second reading), this is what the witness bears when his testimony comes from the Spirit: love, joy, peace, patience, kindness, generosity, faithfulness, humility, self-control . . . (Gal 5:22ff.).

And the Spirit Himself invites us today "to broaden our vision in order to ponder his activity in every time and place" (*Redemptoris Missio* 29). We can all testify to this, even more so in the painful situation in which we find ourselves. Many around us triumph over the forces of evil and despair because they possess peace and patience, humility, justice, self-control, and selflessness. . . . They are hidden, like the Spirit in God; they are often silent; the Spirit has no voice. . . . When they emerge, it is because we need witness-markers on our journey. So it is with Sheikh Bouslimani, an Islamist militant and the driving force behind a kind of Muslim *Caritas*. When extremists urged him to issue a *fatwa* (judgment) authorizing violence in the name of Islam, he chose instead to face arrest, torture, and ultimately death. For all of us, he is a witness because he refused to sin "against the Holy Spirit" [Mt 12:31]. We attest that his "martyrdom" comes from the Spirit, and we proclaim that this scholar of Islamic law shared in the grace of the simple and the little ones, which is to bear witness to the truth.

Thus, Islam is not mistaken when it inscribes the name *shahîd* among the ninety-nine most beautiful names of God. God is the witness *par excellence*. The particularity of this Witness, the Qur'an states, is that He is self-sufficient (mentioned eight times in the Qur'an). This means that there is no need for "two or three witnesses" when it is God who testifies [Mt 18:16]. In fact, this unique Witness is the Holy Spirit; and He testifies that in God, there are two witnesses, the Father and the Son! He presents Himself to us as the Witness of both, and this is His way of introducing us to the love that unites them. "This is my beloved Son," attests the Father, but it is the Spirit who allows us to hear it [Mt 17:5]. "Abba! Father!" attests the Son, but it is the Spirit who whispers it, in Him as in us [Mt 14:36]. His own Passover is to move from one to the other in complete selflessness.

The specific characteristic of this witness, Jesus tells us, is that he has nothing of his own, nothing that belongs to him (Jn 16:13). He receives everything; he gives everything, not withholding anything. The witness of the Spirit is the spirit of poverty. One must have a heart of poverty to bear witness according to the Holy Spirit. Man was created by God, willed by the Father, with that kind of heart, the heart of a son. Pentecost is the rebirth of that vocation. The fearful apostles, whom we see confined in prayer, have made a journey, recognizing themselves overwhelmed in the face of a mission too great for them, expecting everything from God, even the first word of their testimony, and awaiting God from God, so that it may be He who bears witness. And the miracle will be born from the encounter of two poverties, that of the apostles and that of the crowd, present, waiting. In this event, everyone seems to bear witness, each in his own language and according to his own grace.

When we think about our brother Henri and our sister Paule-Hélène—and how can we not think about them?—we know that their witness cannot be separated from what all those who have long benefited from their truly given lives tell us about them. They both came with a heart of poverty, ready to receive, and they confessed to receiving much from this multitude of poor people who weep for them with us, attesting that they owe them a great deal. The Spirit thus created the "bond of peace" [Eph 4:3], and it is He who helps us live their sacrifice as a Pentecost by proclaiming "the wonders of God" upon them and with them [Acts 2:11].

I leave the last word to Henri, from a meeting of our *Ribât* a year ago: "We are all inhabited by the Spirit. . . . God journeys with this people, with this religion [of Islam], but I don't understand (I am like Mary). I am still searching in that regard. I let myself be questioned, and I question. I unsettle the other person a little, and the other person unsettles me. We must always try to discover what is positive in each person and encourage it. Being watchers also means being awakeners, helping people live according to the Spirit."

Untitled
April 13, 1995—Holy Thursday,
Year C (Fez, Morocco)

Texts: Exodus 12:1–8, 11–14;
1 Corinthians 11:23–26; John 13:1–15

Christian de Chergé delivered this 1995 Holy Thursday homily, with its striking hymn-like opening and meditative style, at the monastery's annex in Fez, Morocco. As readers will have noticed, fraternity is a central category in de Chergé's spirituality and theology. In becoming flesh, the Word received a universal range of brothers and sisters, including Abel and Cain, Peter and Judas, and the Peter and Judas "in me." The Word is therefore equally committed to the "brothers of the plain," that is, the soldiers in the Algerian army, and the "brothers of the mountain," that is, the Islamist revolutionaries. The reciprocal nature of the Incarnation, which de Chergé emphasizes also in his chapter talks of the same period, means that fraternity has been introduced into God as well. Thus, when the monks persevere in their call to fraternal love, to serving one another and their neighbors in everyday, ordinary acts of love, they are truly participating in the divine offering of Christ to his Father.

> He loved me to the end, the end of me,
> the end of him . . . [see Jn 13:1]

He loved me in his own way, which is not mine.

He loved me graciously, gratuitously. . . . Perhaps I would have liked it to be more discreet, less solemn.

He loved me as I do not know how to love: the simplicity, the self-forgetfulness, the humble and un-gratifying service, without any self-regard.

He loved me with the benevolent but inescapable authority of a father, and also with the forbearing and concerned tenderness of a mother.

I was wounded at the heel by the common enemy [Gn 3:15], and there [Jesus] is at my feet: "Do not be afraid, all is pure." Like Peter, I am ashamed. It has happened to me too, stumbling while following him, and even raising my heel against him because there is a little Judas in me, and I strongly want to seek refuge in the night, especially when the Light is there, probing my darkness. Fortunately, he only looks at my feet, and my eyes can look away.

Will the water he poured cause me to weep?

I dreamed of love as a fusion of myself with Him, but it is a transfusion that I need: his blood in my blood, his flesh in my flesh, his Heart in mine, the real presence of man walking in the presence of the Father.

Poverty, chastity, and obedience find in me a compliant son.

Alas! Love was revealed, but it is already slipping away from me. He was there, at my feet, all mine. I couldn't hold onto him.

He passes to the feet of my neighbor and to Judas himself, to all those of whom one does not know whether they truly are disciples, whom I've had to accept; it was the price of staying with Him, and of having the right, this evening, to the bread and the cup.

He loved his own to the end, all of his own; they are all his, each one as unique, a multitude of unique ones.

God loved us so much that he gave us his only One: and the Word became BROTHER, the brother of Abel and also of Cain, the brother of both Isaac and Ishmael, the brother of Joseph and the eleven others who sold him, the brother of the plain and the brother of the mountain, the brother of Peter, of Judas, and of both in me.

The Hour has come for God to learn what it costs to enter into fraternity. An only Son, he had come (from God). Brother to the infinity of men, he returns to God, leading the multitude to the end of the Unique One.

"I have given you an example" [Jn 13:15]: The lesson is there, on the table, with this bread and this cup to share, but the teacher's manual is the gesture of a servant, heart and body surrendered, there, from foot to foot, from brother to brother, engraving the memory.

"My brother, my sister, and my mother, they are the ones who will do to the least of my brothers what I did there with you" [see Mt 12:50].

Nothing is purer from now on than an assembly of brothers loving one another, growing closer and closer, to the extreme of patience and compassion, so that no one is lost among those that JESUS, our brother, offers this evening to his Father, like his own Body and Blood.

"You Are the Other Whom We Await"
December 10, 1995
2nd Sunday of Advent, Year A

Texts: Isaiah 11:1–10, "The wolf shall
   be a guest of the lamb . . ."
Romans 15:4–9, "Welcome one another . . ."
Matthew 3:1–12, "The one who is coming
   after me is mightier than I . . ."

Readers familiar with the thought of the philosopher Emmanuel Levinas (1906–1995) will recognize here his influence on Christian de Chergé's understanding of the "Wholly Other." In the other, in every other, even in those who pose a threat, the potential exists for recognizing the presence of the Wholly Other. Only a few months before the monks were abducted, de Chergé returns here to the importance of unity-in-difference, its divine-Trinitarian origin and its created expressions.

Notes: The mention of Saint-Brieuc, a town in Brittany, France, refers to the nearby Trappist Abbey of Melleray. "God is God, and there is no other" is a play on the first part of the Islamic testimony of faith (shahâda)*: There is no god but God* (La ilaha illallah)*. On Sr. Odette Prévost, see the introduction to the chapter talk of November 28, 1995.*

You are the Other whom we await. . . . This theme proposed for the whole of ADVENT (see the liturgical handouts of Saint-Brieuc) can help us, it seems to me, fruitfully to interpret the readings of this Sunday. The anxious expectation of "The awaited Other" runs throughout all of Scripture. It inscribes itself like a watermark into the fabric of each of our lives, which are marked by successive encounters and waitings.

The other, wholly other, offers himself to us as a possible companion on the human adventure, as the endearing friend, as the brother whom we would miss, able to share with us bread and salt on the journey of life.

The other, wholly other, also presents himself as the stranger whose resemblance often turns out to be misleading, a seducer inclined to see us as "other," like himself, and thus to alter us in a fundamental way; sometimes he is even an adversary ready to test our limits.

Thus, where there is no mutual respect for what each one is, we run the threat of a conflict of identities, with the risk of distorting the other, or of letting oneself be assimilated by him, of effacing or of being effaced. One could quickly become the lamb for a wolf, but the reverse is also quite possible!

However, in the extraordinary richness of creation, as within the diversity of people themselves, God has prepared us to welcome difference. This is an essential component of all love. Even more so when this love is expressed and lived in the very image of the One from whom it emanates. An inscrutable mystery of this One-in-Three God, where the

Spirit ceaselessly lives the difference, between the Father and the Son first of all, and then little by little between each one and other among us.

In the testimony that our sister ODETTE gave last year, namely, the personal reasons that led her to the decision to remain in Algeria despite the turmoil and the violence, she stated firmly: "TO STAY is to affirm our fundamental human right, the right to DIFFERENCE (with recognition of this right among the Algerians themselves in their own diversity)." Those who assassinated ODETTE and so many others sought to eliminate their "difference." But we must continue to affirm that this "right to difference" is good news for the world. That is our "gospel."

In our first reading (Isa 11:1–10), it is the SPIRIT who, first of all, discerns this "shoot from the stump of Jesse," already heavy with many generations [Isa 11:1]. A shoot that distinguishes himself from others, first because he proclaims, among men, the difference of God. No, it is no longer possible to give in to the illusion of the Tempter, pressing man to erase the radical difference: "You will be like gods!" [Gn 3:5]. Sin is there from the beginning. JESUS comes to proclaim that *God is God, and there is no other*. He also comes as the MAN who, in our midst, will live differently . . . because he burns with the FIRE of a love that unites without consuming.

With him rises the new world announced by Isaiah, where difference no longer imposes itself as an instigator of war and discord. A harmony is possible in this world of beasts, where man puts on such a good face, with the hatreds and fears of which he is capable. It's a prophetic vision of a world where "the wolf and the lamb live together" or "the cow and the bear shall graze together. . . ." It's not an undifferentiated world: the viper remains a viper, and "the baby shall play by the cobra's den" without trying to displace it or to move in [Isa 11:6–8]. Something has changed in the order of relationships—namely, the very thing that was wounded in mutual relations, which is called EVIL under all its forms.

The CONVERSION called for by John the Baptist at the threshold of a new era is announced as a DIFFERENCE to be respected and introduced into one's life. He sets the example himself: he changes his place, clothing, diet . . . , and the crowds join him; all the categories are flummoxed. Even the Pharisees and the Sadducees, sworn enemies, present themselves together. John violently rails against them. This coalition of supposed "children of Abraham" is false. Is it not in their relations with each other that they should demonstrate the "fruits of conversion"? [Mt 3:9–10]. [Conversion] begins with a profound interior change that conveys the meaning of LOVE, with its multifaceted richness, upon their obvious and legitimate differences, and the sense of an open communion, through the attraction of opposites and the complementarity of the gifts given to each and every one.

This mutual welcome marks the world inaugurated by Jesus Christ as Saint PAUL sees it (second reading): Jews and pagans, all children of Abraham from now on can take their place in the concert of languages and nations, "with one accord, with one voice," glorifying the One Lord [Rom 15:6].

Paul also says that to attain this result requires "COURAGE and ENDURANCE" [Rom 15:4–5].

The courage to continue to be oneself in a world that levels everything, in a world of exclusion and multiple fundamentalisms. John himself doesn't want us to be mistaken: "No, I am not the one . . . ! I am not the Messiah, nor Elijah, nor the Prophet. . . ." I am not the other, "the other whom you await." I am only "the voice" of the other [Jn 1:20–23].

The courage also to accept the other as they are, where they are, with their gifts, their limitations, their distinctiveness, without desiring them to be what we are, or what we would like them to be. Trust must prevail, even if there is room for doubt. It is John who, from his prison, will send the question to Jesus: "Are you the one who is to come?" The Messiah, whom we imagined differently? Or, "Must we await another?" [Mt 11:3].

The courage, in fact, to be only water when the other is fire. Without trying to extinguish the fire, as water might. Without fear that this Fire might evaporate me: it is not there for that!

Before the paradise described in the prophetic images of Isaiah, before the definitive establishment of the coming of the Kingdom where we will finally understand the "Why?" of our differences (Q 5:48); now is the time for awaiting the Other.

It is above all a time of MERCY. It is up to us to receive it with gratitude from the Wholly Other, as hidden witnesses of the difference that Jesus introduced by coming into the world, "the light that shines in our darkness" [Jn 1:5]. "The spirit of wisdom and strength, of counsel and discernment, of knowledge and fear of the Lord" presides over this difference toward which he orients all [the differences] of the "others," including my own, in their waiting for the Other: difference, my HOPE! [Isa 11:2].

Yes, truly, Lord, you are the OTHER whom we await!

Articles

Although most of Christian de Chergé's writing appears as chapter talks, homilies, and responses to directives from the Cistercian Order or the local church, he also wrote a dozen or so longer and more academic articles that he delivered as addresses and/or published in various journals. The three chosen for this collection represent the early, middle, and later stages of his career, but they display a remarkable consistency. Each article weaves together the author's Christian commitments, openness to Islam, and key personal narratives. He never drops his monastic lens, "reading" both the Qur'an and the wider Islamic tradition through the practice of lectio divina *and encouraging "disarmed hearts" toward "reciprocal conversion." His appreciation for the "Islam of hearts" remains steadfast across the thirteen years represented here.*

Praying in the Church: Listening to Islam (1982)

Notes: In "Praying in the Church. Listening to Islam," the phrase not more than one *translates* ne font pas nombre. *It's a difficult expression that de Chergé employs to indicate distinction within an underlying unity. In this case, he recognizes that Muslim and Christian understandings of God are different, but that fact, he asserts, does not make for more than one God. The "lovers of God" to whom de Chergé refers are the brothers of the Alawiyya Sufi confraternity who joined the Ribât dialogues. Brother Roger Schutz (1915–2005) was the founder and prior of the Taizé ecumenical monastic community, whose spirituality deeply influenced Christian de Chergé.*

The "Opinion" titled "Regarding Islam" hit me hard (*Tychique* 34 [November 1981]: 48–55). I am still shocked by what, to my mind, such a piece represents in a "journal of formation" intended for prayer groups. Can one really promote, even under the rubric of free opinion, a "theological" contribution that is so distant, both in its spirit and its

---

"Prier en Église. À l'écoute de l'Islam" originally appeared as a reader-reaction in *Tychique* 34 (1982): 48–55. It was republished in Christian de Chergé, *Lettres à un ami fraternel*, ed. Maurice Borrmans (Montrouge, France: Bayard Éditions, 2015), 180–89. It also appeared in *Chemins de dialogue* 27 (2006): 17–24. Our translation is based upon the Bayard publication.

terms, from what the Church has been striving to help us discover, especially since Vatican II, by probing more deeply the meaning and values of the enormous reality of the non-Christian world?

And how can this article by a "missionary priest in North Africa" be reconciled with the perspectives of encounter developed by the bishops of the same region, especially in their lengthy pastoral letter of 1979 (*Documentation catholique* 79, 1032–44)?

However, my strongest reaction is less about this unwelcome article than about the unfortunate little statement adopted by the 1981 "Open Door" convention (highlighted in the same issue of *Tychique*): "Today we invite you to pray that all our Churches share a common vision regarding the work of evangelization in the Muslim world. This implies that each Church would obey the Lord's command and submit to the Father's will, who desires that all men be saved."

If the intention is to pray that the attitude and opinion expressed by our "missionary priest" be shared in the Church, it seems vital for me to break the silence, even monastic silence, in order to cry out a completely different echo of intercession that is also rooted in North Africa. In doing so, I will remain within the strict limits of a vocation of prayer that is characterized specifically as being a spiritual presence in the Muslim world. I would like simply to explain, in the form of a very personal testimony, the role of Islam and its people in the journey of one brother striving to be Christian. It's a matter of justice.

It has been forty years, this very year, that, for the first time, I saw men praying differently than my elders. I was five years old, and I was discovering Algeria during a first stay of three years. I remain deeply grateful to my mother, who taught my brother and me to respect the integrity and rites of this Muslim prayer. "They are praying to God," my mother said. Thus, I have always known that the God of Islam and the God of Jesus Christ are not more than one. Such is the language of the Church, from Gregory VII (1076) to John Paul II, who very recently stated in Nigeria, "All of us, Christians and Muslims, live under the sun of the One Merciful God. We both believe in One God who is the creator of man. We adore God and profess total submission to Him. Thus, in the true sense, we can call one another *brothers and sisters in faith in the one God*" (*Documentation catholique* 1982, 244–45).

About twenty-five years ago I rediscovered this country [Algeria] and those who pray in this country. Having reached adulthood and confronted, like my entire generation, the harsh reality of the conflict of the time, I had the chance to meet a mature and deeply religious man who liberated my faith by teaching me to live it amidst the challenges of daily life as a response of simplicity, openness, and surrender to God. Our dialogue was that of a peaceful and trusting friendship that had God's will as its horizon, above the fray. This unlettered man did not hide behind words. Unwilling to betray one group for the sake of another, either his brothers or his friends, he risked his own life, despite being responsible for his ten children. He expressed this gift concretely when he sought to protect, in a skirmish with his brothers, a friend who was more at risk than him. Knowing his life was threatened he accepted my humble promise to "pray for him." He simply remarked, "I know you will pray for me . . . but, you see, Christians do not know how to pray. . . ." I perceived in this comment a reproach addressed to a Church that did not yet present itself, at least legibly, as a community of prayer.

In the blood of this friend, I knew that my call to follow Christ would need to be lived out, sooner or later, in the very country where this pledge of the greatest love was given to me. I knew, at the same time, that this consecration of my life would have to involve *prayer in common* in order truly to be a witness of the Church.

Thus began a pilgrimage toward the communion of saints where Christians and Muslims, and many others, share the same filial joy. For I know that I can set in the place where my hope leads at least one Muslim, this beloved brother who lived the imitation of Jesus Christ even in his death. And every Eucharist renders him infinitely close to me, in the reality of the Body of glory where the gift of his life has revealed its full significance, "for me and for the many."

Returning to my own, I knew that I did not have to teach them a lesson in prayer, but also that the small "monastic Church" to which I attached myself would have to grow in its unique vocation as a praying presence among others who pray, sharing in all of daily life in order to be, with immense and joyful hope, a visible sign of the Kingdom.

I joined this small monastery without knowing either its exact location or the brothers. It was enough for me [to know] that it was in this country and among these Muslims, whom the very call to the Liturgy of the Hours led me to welcome from Christ, He, "who intercedes ceaselessly on our behalf" [Heb 7:25]. They would be another community that I would need to learn to understand and to contemplate in its most authentic "Islam," that is to say, in its surrender to God. And this with no other desire than that of "mutual conversion" destined to lead us together, and, if it pleases God, one group through the other, to each one's definitive place in the grand assembly of all the living.

The monastic vow of *conversion of life* lends a particular

meaning and support on which I believed I could base my own definitive commitment, confidently proclaiming on the day of my profession:

> Monastic praise and Muslim prayer have a spiritual kinship that I wish to learn to celebrate more, under the gaze of the One who, Alone, calls us to prayer, and who undoubtedly asks us, mysteriously, *together* to be the "salt of the earth" [Mt 5:13]. What's more, certain religious values of Islam are an undeniable inspiration for the monk, in line with his vocation. This includes the gift of oneself, surrender to the Word, Pilgrimage, almsgiving, conversion of heart, trust in Providence, hospitality.... In all of this, I strive to recognize the Spirit of Holiness, of whom no one knows from where it comes or where it goes....

Thus, I saw clearly, from the outset, that a contemplative vocation would have to express itself here as a demanding fidelity to the Christ of the Gospels, attentive to discovering signs of the Kingdom and the action of the Spirit outside the visible boundaries of the chosen people.... The realization of evangelical values nourished by Muslim faith came alive within me.

I was then able to resume Arabic studies and to engage in a more systematic study of Islam. My reading of the Qur'an, already undertaken for a long time, was greatly facilitated. I found many biblical images there, which my Hebrew studies had made quite familiar to me.

Certainly, the *Word of God* [*Parole de Dieu*] is one, eternally spoken by the Word [*Verbe*], in the silence of the Spirit. But the echoes it has sounded in history and that it inexhaustibly arouses in upright hearts appear infinitely diverse. For a long time, we turned a deaf ear to the message of the other, challenging its original connection to the Wholly Other. We continue to clash, sometimes harshly, in the name of these differences.

And yet, the One who opens the path of the Scriptures for us is also the One who wishes to keep us hungry for every Word [*Parole*] that comes from the mouth of the Most High. Just as it is possible to undertake a *lectio divina* of nature, of every creature, and of the human heart, similarly, I believe a contemplative can let the Book of Islam resonate, in the peace of an interior listening, with the desire and respect of those brothers who draw from it their taste for God. Gamaliel's advice (Acts 5:39) surely applies to Islam after fifteen centuries of existence, and thus to the Qur'an. With regular reading, the Qur'an gradually ceases to seem so dry, even if it often remains challenging and unsettling, just as many biblical passages do. At the point where I am, I understand how Pastor J. P. Gabus could write: "I believe profoundly that Islam is rooted in the tradition of Judeo-Christian revelation and that Muhammad was a prophet genuinely inspired by the Spirit of the One and Living God" (*Tychique* 28 [November 1980]).

In fact it has happened to me often enough that I discover while reading the Qur'an one of those Emmaus journeys where the joy that burns in the heart of our God vibrates. Some of the verses I like to ruminate on seem to offer a shortcut of the Gospel, always with a new and relevant meaning. But through them the conviction anchored within me remains deeply attuned to my faith, affirming that the Christ of Easter fulfills all Scriptures, including the Qur'an.

This long apprenticeship to another Word [*Parole*] from a "God who reveals" (see *Nostra Aetate*) has been wonderfully supported by the unknown friends who knocked on our door one day and undertook to journey with me for a while.

I think of M., who, seven years ago already, was the first to ask me to accompany him in a spontaneous prayer. For three hours, our voices joined and supported each other, merging into praise of the One from whom all love is born: an experience so close to what I had tasted through the Charismatic Renewal in its early days (1972–1974). Since then, others have taken the same initiative. Each time, what a discovery, what a coming together!

And how can we forget those who live, with a free heart, the obligations of their religious belonging, like M., who said to me, on the eve of last Ramadan: "You see, the fast (of Ramadan) is a gift from God that draws us to Him"! The word of a simple man who has never "read" the Scriptures. . . . It's also an authentic definition of the Cross and the Eucharist.

And then, for the past two years, there have been these brothers who call themselves "lovers of God" and who are bound to each other by a commitment of daily fraternal support, on the same spiritual path, within the school of a master. They wanted to join us as a monastic community in a journey of common prayer. Other gatherings have followed, with sharing around themes involving our relationship with God: remembrance or prayer of the heart (*dhikr*), covenant, fraternal love. . . . One of them, a heating technician, said to me one day: "The Holy Spirit? You know, we shouldn't try too hard to understand it; that takes away its allure!"

Thus there is a fraternal listening to Islam that can lead us back to the very heart of the mystery of God, in a humble attachment to a Christ who is always greater than what we can express and live by. In a journal, Brother Roger Schutz noted on September 10, 1974: "I affirmed to Hassan last night: your presence is the assurance that soon we will no longer be able to speak of the love of God without discovering the treasures of trust in Him contained in your family of origin, Islam" (*The Wonder of a Love*, Taizé, 1979).

We must be clear! If I have the audacity of hoping to signify, in this *living together*, something of the communion of saints, it is first and foremost because I learn, personally, and day after day, that God's plan for Christianity, as well as for Islam, remains to invite us all to the *table of sinners*. The multiplied bread that we are already given to break together is the absolute trust in the unique mercy of the Almighty. When we agree to meet in this sharing, doubly brothers because we are "prodigal" and because we are forgiven, it becomes possible, I can attest, to listen to and recognize the one same Word [*Parole*] of God delivering its richness of life, the one same Word [*Verbe*] offered to the multitude for the forgiveness of sins.

In the school of the desert fathers and that of the elders, the monk learns that the path to conversion involves coming to *a greater integrity of life*. We take this path every time we seek to reduce the often-astonishing contrast between our human behavior and our declarations of faith. Without this tireless quest for an authentic interior and performative coherence, there will be no understanding of what unites us with the other, since, as experience has taught me, we always end up encountering the other at the level where we truly seek them. Without personal authenticity, what truth can we dream of communicating?

There is for Christians and Muslims, therefore, a possible path of shared fidelity, one where every human relationship can be lived as an "encounter in love and in truth" (see Ps 84). For, just as love for our brother speaks the truth of our love for God, so too our readiness to recognize and welcome the portion of truth placed in our brother's heart will express, better than any other discourse, our thirst and our love for the Truth that is only in God.

Any dogmatic assertion that does not contribute to engendering a style closer to the experience of men, in the very name of God, strongly risks being nothing but a sterile, blind, and partisan abstraction. Christians and Muslims, we run the same risk in that regard. Nothing is more foreign to the Gospel than a sectarianism incapable of celebrating the faith of the Roman centurion or the charity of the Good Samaritan, solely based on their actions. I know something of the real joy of embracing both in wonder, even as I must confess my weak faith and my lack of love.

So, when it happens that I observe or have to endure certain forms of sectarianism—and it's true, they do exist within the Muslim community—I look elsewhere for the *Islam of hearts*, in the direction of my departed friend, and of so many others who have had or still retain that same pure and insistent human face. And just as some of them consider me one of their own, it is no wonder that I feel them so close to the One who became for me Way, Truth, and Life.

Brother Christian-Marie
A monk in North Africa, Pentecost 1982

The Mystical Ladder
of Dialogue (1989)

In "The Mystical Ladder of Dialogue," de Chergé uses several Islamic terms. On the "House of Islam" (Dâr al-Islâm), *see the introduction to the letter of February 25, 1985. The rightly guided caliphs are the first four leaders of the Islamic community to succeed the Prophet Muhammad after his death in 632: Abû Bakr (573–634), 'Umar ibn al-Khattâb (583–644), Uthmân ibn Affân (573–656), and Ali ibn Abi Tâlib (600–661). After the death of Ali, civil war broke out between groups eventually identified as Sunni and Shi'a Muslims over claims of succession.* Hegira *refers to the emigration of the Prophet Muhammad and his early followers from Mecca to Medina in 622 to avoid persecution; it marks the first year of the Islamic calendar. A* muezzin *is the Muslim who calls his fellow Muslims to prayer at the prescribed hours. Of the same root as* djem'â *is* masjid, *the Muslim place of prayer, often called a* mosque *in the West. De Chergé's inclusion of* ladder/sullam *as sharing a root meaning with* peace/salaam *and* surrender/islam *may rely more on colloquial usage than on technical etymology. Salman Rushdie (b. 1947) is a British Indian writer whose novel* The Satanic Verses *(1988) sparked the controversy to which de Chergé refers. The Ayatollah Khomeini was*

"L'échelle mystique du dialogue" was originally delivered as a talk in Rome at the *Journées romaines* of 1989 (see the introduction to the letter of June 26, 1985). It was revised by de Chergé and published posthumously by the editors in *Islamochristiana* 23 (1996): 1–26.

the supreme leader of Iran (1979–1989). Rushdie was forced into hiding for many years, and in 2022 he was nonfatally stabbed by an attacker. Finally, de Chergé refers to prayer and work as two mamelles *of Benedictine life. Literally,* mamelles *means breasts, teats, or* mammary glands. *While the image of nourishment is certainly important, we decided to employ a more familiar English idiom, describing prayer and work as the two lungs of Benedictine life.*

> Indeed, we had accepted within ourselves the sentence of death, that we might trust not in ourselves but in God who raises the dead. He rescued us from such great danger of death . . . in him we have put our hope that he will also rescue us again! (2 Cor 1:9–10)

"Those who pray among those who pray. . . ." That's how we defined ourselves in 1975, even though we had eight days to leave the place . . . [the place] where we are still. Isn't that already a kind of answer to the question that occupies us during these *Journées*: "What is our common social project?"

I will speak as a witness, but we must not forget that it's a communal witness, even if it's true that as guest master and prior, roles which were given to me by my brothers, I have found myself at the forefront of our encounter and sharing. Nothing can be understood apart from the common presence and fidelity of all of us to our humble daily reality, from the garden gate to the kitchen, to *lectio divina*.

Thus a particular mode of dialogue has taken root here, an essential characteristic of which is the fact that we never take the initiative. I would readily call it existential. It is often the fruit of a long *living together* and of shared concerns that can be very concrete. This means that it is rarely of a strictly theological order. We tend to avoid that kind of jousting, which I find narrow-minded. . . .

Existential dialogue, which is to say dialogue that is simultaneously manual and spiritual, of the everyday and of the eternal, is such that the men or women who call on us must be welcomed in their concrete and mysterious reality as children of God, "created beforehand in Christ" (Eph 2:10). We would cease to be Christians and, even more simply, human beings if we were to deny the other in his hidden dimension by encountering him only, so-to-speak, "man to man," understood in an impoverished sense as being stripped of any reference to God, of any personal and therefore unique relationship with the Wholly Other. [We prefer] dialogue that keeps its feet on the ground (and even in the manure) but its head seeking above.

That's the view from my spyglass. The reverse view actually, which gives a narrow perspective, but I would add that this telescope often works at night, and that's important. One might conclude: "He's dreaming!" Dreams? It is true that the monastic vocation is more directly related to the prophetic function of the Church, a function that our Churches immersed in the *House of Islam* must faithfully appropriate, as John Paul II underscored four years ago with the Christians of Morocco:

> What you are deepening here in a natural way can lead to significant development, by building bridges elsewhere among different traditions. This constitutes one form of service in the vocation of the Christians of Morocco, in a world where respectful dialogue is not always easy. ["Homily," Charles de Foucauld Institute, Casablanca, Morocco, August 19, 1985, *Documentation catholique*, 1903 (October 6, 1985): 940]

I. HOPE BY ANOTHER NAME

Between realization and possibility, faith tells us there is room for an unseen *third world* of *hope*. However, there's no avoiding the shared evidence that we cannot serve two masters. Once we've rendered to Caesar all that's legitimately due, we must still "render" Caesar to God. Caesar can be many things, and God knows he is, but that must not divert us from striving to build together a world ordered to the One who, hope tells us, will lead us to His Shore. If the monk believes he has anything to say here, it is less as an efficient builder of the city of Men (although . . .) than as a resolute adept of a way of being in the world that would have no meaning apart from what we call the *last things* of hope (eschatology).

Along this long journey, the pitfalls that threaten us are well known. I count three:

1. *The Myth of the Golden Age*

There is a tendency to search the past for the perfect model of society that it would suffice to restore for everything to become paradise again. A "Christian" paradise perhaps for those who are nostalgic for the early days of the Church as described in the Acts of the Apostles: "They devoted themselves to the teaching of the Apostles, to the common life, to the breaking of bread and to the prayers" (Acts 2:42; see also Acts 4:32–35; 5:12–14).

Similarly, one could return to the ideal Muslim community, that of the first State of Medina perfectly organized by the Prophet or that of the first four *rightly guided* caliphs and the miraculous expansion of Islam that occurred almost without firing a shot:

> History shows that at that time no coercion was used to convert subjugated peoples. It was rather the

simplicity of their spiritual doctrine and the perfect honesty of the conquerors that made an impression. [Muhammad Hamidullah, *Initiation à l'Islam* (El Menzah, Tunisia: Tunisie éditions, 1990), no. 496, p. 188]

Faith sprang forth naturally from the reading of the Book: tears of joy. One thinks of the feats and miracles that characterized our desert fathers and, closer to home, of the beginning of *Cîteaux* as described to us by the Order's tradition:

> The brothers, seeing that possessions and virtues do not ordinarily go together for long, choosing to serve the poor Christ in poverty, preferred to be occupied with heavenly exercises rather than involved in temporal affairs. . . . They ventured toward the desert of Cîteaux, then a place of dread and immense loneliness. . . . Believing that the harshness of the place suited their project well, they supposed that the place had been prepared for them by God, and it became as pleasant as the project was dear to them. (*Exorde* of Cîteaux)

Sure, but . . . it was not long before these valiant founders were requesting assistance. Benedict narrowly escaped being poisoned by his first "comrades" from Vicovaro. Three of the four caliphs died violent deaths. Nor was dissent lacking in the apostolic age over questions of observance, simony, and parochialism.

2. The Trial of Modernity

Once denounced as a "satanic" theme, modernity now appears unavoidable. In fact the Church at Vatican II sought to position itself resolutely "in the world of today" (*Gaudium et Spes*). We can still hear the solemn appeal of Paul VI to the United Nations in October 1965:

> The hour has come when a pause, a moment of recollection, reflection, you might say of prayer, is absolutely needed so that we may think back over our common origin, our history, our common destiny. The appeal to the moral conscience of man has never before been as necessary as it is today, in an age marked by such great human progress. For the danger comes neither from progress nor from science; if these are used well they can, on the contrary, help to solve a great number of the serious problems besetting mankind. The real danger comes from man, who has at his disposal ever more powerful instruments that are as well fitted to bring about ruin as they are to achieve lofty conquests. ["Address to the U.N.," October 4, 1965, *Documentation catholique*, no. 1457, October 17, 1965, col. 1730]

In a recent thesis, an Algerian academic echoes this message by denouncing the absence of contemplation, the ravages of which could be incalculable:

> Modernity compels the believer (whether Christian or Muslim) to reread his fundamental sources and to meditate both on the meaning of revelation and the demands of the times. (*Pro manuscripto*, 1988, p. 420)

It's no longer fitting for man, whoever he is, to rely solely on the tradition of what has always been said or what has always been done. He must learn to conceive of himself, and to evolve, on a planetary scale if he hopes to be honest with his fellow men, and therefore with himself and with his faith.

Moreover, we live in a time that constantly confronts us, all of us, with problems that were not broached as such by our respective Scriptures. Many Muslims now consider as insufficient and outdated the assertion that the Qur'an foresaw all the developments of science (bioethics, chemical weapons, brainwashing, etc.). What Word of God [*Parole de Dieu*] might we discover [in that realization] today?

Let us remember that Islam presented itself to us in this way [i.e., as an unforeseen development]. We quickly rejected it as an invention of the devil, arguing that the New Testament had not explicitly foreseen it. Revelation closed. Modernity and its specific concerns, by inviting us to seek today's way through the letter of yesterday, may help us to become better readers of the Muslim reality. Wouldn't that be more rooted in the Christian message than the thinking of Christianity has sometimes been? To comprehend better may demand that we find ourselves together, naked and vulnerable, in the midst of our contemporaries' probing interrogations. A challenge has been leveled at us:

> It contains the reproach often addressed to certain religious men, not for being religious, but for being insufficiently so; not for being Christian, but for not truly being so. [Jean Daniélou, *L'Oraison, problème politique* (Paris: Fayard, 1965), 46]

3. The Demons of Fundamentalism

A third pitfall is undoubtedly on everyone's mind. It's the matter of fundamentalism, the demons of which have suddenly woken up, here and there, including within our little monastic world. To make the danger and its consequences tangible, all we need to do is revisit the drama that played out before a shocked world between last February 14th and 19th.

On February 14th, Imam Khomeini orders that the writer Salman Rushdie be "promptly executed." On the 18th, the author "deeply regrets the pain caused to the sincere believers of Islam." On the 19th, having learned of the regret, the imam insists that Rushdie "must be sent to hell . . . even if he repents." Since then the imam has died. If in his own last moments [Khomeini] had to make the choice left to an elderly David [1 Chr 21:7–13], we can bet that his wish too would have been to fall into the hands of God rather than those of men. Did he feel the rising fear that we all suddenly felt of falling into the hands of his emulators? Those of our Churches, it is true, are they not also stained with innocent blood?

Against the resurgent temptations of fundamentalism and legalism, so incongruous with an evangelical landscape, we must remain at all costs the witnesses of the impossible commandment: "Even if we have faith to move mountains, if we lack love, we are nothing, zero" [see 1 Cor 13:1]. But when have we truly loved? I can hear a Muslim friend asking in echo: "When have we really applied the *sharî'a*?" Paul understood well that the Law condemns to slavery because it makes the inevitable transgressions that much more obvious (see his Letter to the Galatians).

4. A Middle Way . . . ?

Between the pitfalls mentioned, the common reflex will be to find a *middle way*, understood as one accessible to all as well as reasonable in its objectives. Islam gladly offers itself as a religion of moderation. It even becomes a dogma: "God obliges no one beyond his capacity" (Q 2:286). "Thus did we make you a middle community" (Q 2:143). Or again, even about the Ramadan fast, it is written: "God desires ease for you, he does not desire hardship for you" (Q 2:185). Hence the judgment often heard:

> The merit of Islam is to have discovered the things that it is important for every man to share and to practice in common as a necessary minimum, a minimum which affects both the spiritual and material needs of man. [Hamidullah, *Initiation à l'Islam*, no. 203, p. 76]

We must not let ourselves be impressed by the feeling that Christ opened up a path that most people, including us, cannot easily follow. There is in the Gospel a constant requirement to take into account the strengths of each person and not to place heavy burdens on the shoulders of others (Mt 23:4ff.). Likewise, Saint Benedict doesn't believe he's failed by writing only a "very small Rule, written for beginners" (*Rule*, chap. 73).

Let us agree that, by placing too much emphasis on the ideal, we have given the impression that we [already] achieved it with the grace of baptism. Each in turn, Christians and Muslims have betrayed any sense of proportion by presenting themselves as being definitively "the best."

5. A Beyond, under the Sign of the Times

The more immense the hope, the higher the ladder, the more we know instinctively that it will be realized only by resolutely and patiently committing ourselves over the long term. We will have to live [our hope] one day at a time in order to maintain it. All our little gestures will speak of it. A cup of water offered or received, a morsel of bread shared, a helping hand, will tell more accurately than a theology manual about what it's possible for us to be together.

We are marked, all of us, by the call of a *beyond*, but the logic of this beyond is first of all that there is *more to do* between us, today, together. A new world is in gestation, and it is incumbent upon us to reveal its soul.

The Judgment of this world has already begun, and it touches us where we reveal ourselves to be incapable of fidelity to each other:

> Go away from me, cursed ones, to the eternal fire . . . for I was hungry, and you gave me nothing to eat, I was thirsty, I was naked, sick, in prison, and you did nothing. . . . (Mt 25:41ff.)

We also read:

> What led you into the blazing Fire? And (the sinners) answer: We were not among those who pray, we did not feed the poor, we argued in vain with the lovers of disputes; we treated the Day of Judgment as a lie. (Q 74:40–46)

For thirty years, I have carried the existence of Islam within me like a burning question, and I have had an immense curiosity about the place it holds in the mysterious plan of God. Death alone, I think, will provide me with the awaited answer. I am certain that I will come to understand it, dazzled in the paschal light of Him who presents himself to me as the only possible *Muslim* because he is totally *yes* to the will of the Father. I am convinced, however, that by allowing this question to haunt me, I am learning to discover better, here and now, the connections and even the convergences, including those of faith. And I am also learning not to constrain the other according to some idea I have of him—which perhaps my Church transmitted to me—not even according to what he may currently, or typically, say about himself. The exception interests me as well. Are we going to say, effectively, that the monk is not a *true* Christian solely on the pretext that he is in fact rather *rare* in Christianity?

6. Pilgrims of the Horizon

It seems to me that to live in the *House of Islam* is acutely to feel the difficulty, and therefore the urgency, of some original features of the Gospel that the Church has only recently extracted from her treasury (at the turn of Vatican II): nonviolence, demand for justice, religious freedom, refusal of proselytism, spirituality of dialogue, respect for difference, not to mention solidarity with the poor, which is ever to be rediscovered. Likewise, it would be contrary to the Gospel to take these new steps toward the other only on the condition that he himself does the same. We sometimes hear it said: "We are always the ones who take the lead." Now stop! As if we are not already indebted to the awesome initiative of the One who "loved us to the end" [Jn 13:1]. We must abandon at all costs this *tit-for-tat* retaliation, which still haunts us in a thousand ways. Going toward the other and going toward God, it's all one, and I can't live without it. Each requires the same gratuity.

Our mission thus takes up another purpose, which [Jürgen] Moltmann defined as "a qualitative change in the atmosphere of life" [*The Church in the Power of the Spirit* (London: SCM Press, 1977), 159].

Because the same horizon is opened to all of us, it is vital that we learn to walk together in the name of what is best in ourselves. A verse says:

> We shall show them our Signs, on the horizons and in themselves. . . . (Q 41:53)

Our Alawiyya brothers of Médéa quoted and commented on this verse at their first meeting with the *Ribât*, on All Saints Day 1980. It seemed to them to ground the initiative they had taken a few months earlier, when they came to pray with our community of Atlas. They declared from the outset:

> We do not want to engage with you in a discussion of dogma. We feel called to unity. In dogma or theology, there are many barriers that are erected by men. Here we wish to leave to God the possibility of creating something new between us. But this can only be done in prayer. . . .

Yes, it is always from beyond the horizon of our reason that God comes to us, no matter our respective faiths. And truly we can expect something new each time we strive to decipher his *signs* on the *horizons* of worlds and hearts, when we begin to listen and to learn in the school of the other, the Muslim in this case. This is indeed the objective of our *Ribât*, which, from its beginnings ten years ago, recognized itself in the intuition of Max Thurian, so close to that of our friends from Médéa:

> The Church is not asked to adopt an attitude of conquest, but rather of presence and friendship. It is important that the Church assumes, alongside Islam, a fraternal presence of men and women who share as much as possible in the life of Muslims, in silence, prayer and friendship. This is how, little by little, what God wants for the relations between the Church and Islam will be realized. [*Tradition et renouveau dans l'Esprit* (Taizé: Presses de Taizé, 1977), 14]

As soon as we intentionally offer ourselves to the slow and purifying transformation of a long *living together*, we live again—as another Pascha, another Exodus, another Hegira (Why not?)—the spiritual adventure of Abraham. Our bishops of North Africa have magnificently communicated this vocation of our churches, so deeply attuned to God's plan for the whole human family, in a little-known pastoral letter of 1977:

> We leave home without knowing where we are going, because God is leading us. Some even have the feeling of having abandoned, by obeying the call, the familiar landscape of the certainties of their early formation and the language in which they once expressed them. But they remain stretched out in hope toward the city to come, like the witnesses of whom the Epistle to the Hebrews speaks: "The gaze fixed on Him who is the originator of faith and brings it to completion" (Heb 11:1–12:2). [*Documentation catholique*, no. 1724, July 17, 1977, col. 67ff.]

7. And Jesus Christ?

He is precisely the great sacrament of this *third world* of hope, the initiator of faith among men and its fulfillment in God, both beyond and within us, hidden from the games of the world by the cloud of divine mystery and by the veil of the Incarnation continued. With Vatican II, we believe that

> the Lord is the end of human history, the point toward which the desires of history and civilization converge, the center of the human race, the joy of all hearts and the fullness of their aspirations. (LG [*Lumen Gentium*] 45.2)

Jesus himself instructed us: "No one knows the Son except the Father . . ." (Mt 11:27). Teilhard [de Chardin] commented on this in his own way:

> I believe the Church is still a child. The Christ in whom she lives is disproportionately greater than she imagines. ["On My Attitude to the Official Church," in *The Heart of Matter* (Harcourt, 1980), 117–18]

Don't we tend to forget that, believing that to be Christian is to know everything about Christ? *God is greater, Allahu Akbar.* Christ also is *greater,* inconceivably greater. To proclaim so in naked faith is the best witness (*shahâda*) offered to his divinity.

II. A SOCIETY ON THE PATH OF SPIRITUAL DEVELOPMENT

Our two faith commitments, thus defined, can be depicted as two parallel poles. Their meeting point is in infinity, although they are fertilized by the same manure: suffering, disease, and death in particular. They are set in the ground, but in a strictly vertical orientation of common hope, that which is still indicated in Islam by the finger of the dying raised toward heaven, and that of the Cross, a tree so high that all the birds of the sky can build their nests in it (and not just the birds!). And the horizon we discussed, we see it best when we are lying on the ground, nose in the air, in the manner of the patriarch Jacob on a beautiful night in the East:

> He had a dream: a ladder rested on the ground, with its top reaching to the heavens; and God's messengers were going up and down on it. (Gn 28:10ff.)

A ladder? But of course. The third world of hope is, like all third worlds, in the process of development, spiritual development in this case. Man is not a monkey content with his perch. He was created standing; he invented the *ladder* [*la scala*] to accompany him on his climbs, with precisely two uprights and rungs between them at more-or-less regular intervals to lend support. Why not imagine climbing it in two single-file rows, this common ladder whose uprights would be our respective faiths? Genesis speaks of angels ascending and descending. The angels occupy the rungs on which we place our feet, symbolizing an intermediate created spiritual world whose proper existence is between the so-called *heavenly* world, that of the mystery of God, and the *terrestrial* world (*dunyâ*), where humans, who are both animal and matter, evolve.

Together we recognize that human nature is also—and primarily—spiritual. Mohamed Talbi writes in a recent book:

> Whether we reduce a man to the material support of his body for the sole purpose of sensory enjoyment or sublimate him so that he is no longer anything but spirit, he instantly ceases to be a man. [Mohamed Talbi and Olivier Clément, *Un respect têtu* (Paris: Nouvelle Cité, 1989), 34]

We agree with him again when he says:

> The uniqueness of man in his material and spiritual bipolarity is like a counterpart to the uniqueness of God.

But these two *uniquenesses* are not effaced by the intimate desire that leads them to wed. Let us contemplate the first fruit of this Covenant, the *new man* who identifies himself with the ladder, uprights and rungs now interchangeable, the truly *deiform man* (Talbi quotes F. Schuon), the cruciform man, from all eternity:

> Amen, Amen I say to you, you will see the sky opened and the angels of God ascending and descending on the Son of Man. (Jn 1:51)

1. *The Monastic Call . . .*

Because this new man presents himself first of all as *alone for the Alone*, here I want to take a detour through monastic life. Is it not a radical quest for the Absolute, independent of time and culture, as John Paul II emphasized on the occasion of the fifteenth centenary of Saint Benedict, in 1980?

> Throughout time, there have been men in every religion who, "trying to face, in various ways, the restlessness of the human heart" (*Nostra Aetate* 2), have experienced in an exceptional way the attraction of the Absolute and the Eternal. (Apostolic Letter *Sanctorum Altrix*).

Therefore I mean to speak here of a monasticism that is historically prior to Christianity, and independent of it—even though it was then spontaneously grafted onto the young trunk of the Church—as a witness to the Absolute that is as strong as martyrdom, which is why it resurfaces in Islam.

Islam was born in the desert; it bears the indelible mark of it. The Prophet himself "was inclined to meditation and solitude" (Talbi, 21). Ritual life tends to place the believer *alone with the Alone*, even in Mecca where pilgrims flock by the hundreds of thousands. The muezzin who calls to prayer speaks in the first-person: "I testify . . ." (*ashhadu*), as in the *shahâda* itself. At the top of his minaret, before there were loudspeakers, he would refer to the light that was maintained day and night in the hermitages whose memory the Qur'an rekindles:

> [This lamp is found] in the houses that God has permitted to be raised, where his name is invoked, where men celebrate his praises at dawn and dusk. No commerce, and no barter distracts them from the remembrance of God, from prayer and alms. (Q 24:36–37)

In parallel one thinks about a sermon of Saint Bernard to his monks:

> Here (at the monastery), you do not have to worry about raising children, pleasing wives, markets, trading, or even food and clothing. . . . The evils of the day and the concerns of life are mostly foreign to you; God has hidden you in the most secret place of his tabernacle. (*Sermones de diversis* II, 1)

Christian monasticism was also born in the desert. The Stranger who tore Abraham from his father's tent and pushed him into the desert did not fail to promise him numerous descendants and a fertile land, but [Abraham] would die *without having witnessed the fulfillment of the promises*. In Islam, as in Christianity, there is the awareness of being, like Abraham, "only strangers and travelers on earth," "aspiring to another homeland," since "God has in fact prepared for them a city" to which all desert roads lead (Heb 11:13ff.).

2. The Exodus of Every lectio divina . . .

The Word of God presents itself to each of us as a viaticum for the crossing of the desert, for the Pascha, the Exodus, the Hegira. The Scriptures are a treasure in which Christians love to seek, day and night, the new and the old. *"Ausculta, o fili . . .*, Listen, son!" Those are the first words of the *Rule* of Saint Benedict. *"Iqra'*, Recite!"—another imperative, which opens the Qur'an and which every Muslim understands as applying to himself. The temptation for both of us is to remain with the literal sense, with a fundamentalist and fixed reading. But many undergo the same exodus: "Incline the ear of your heart!," specifies Saint Benedict. Should we continue to turn a deaf ear to the message of the other, denying on principle its authentic relationship to the Wholly Other?

Our Sufi friends like to quote the Gospel, which they are committed to reading, and we know how many parables and words of Jesus find a vibrant echo in the Muslim environment. Couldn't we let the Book of Islam resonate in the peace of an interior listening, with the desire and respect of these same brothers who draw their taste for God from it?

Indeed, I have often experienced, as emerging from the Qur'an, during an initially arduous and disconcerting reading, a kind of shortcut of the Gospel, which thus becomes a true path of communion with the other and with God. So, just sticking with the *Moses cycle*:

> I made you for myself! (Q 20:20) [20:41]
> My Lord, I hastened unto You, that You may be content. (Q 20:84)
> My Lord, I am in need of any good that You desire for me. (Q 28:24), etc.

It seems to me that the Christ of Easter would have something to tell us about Himself through these verses and many others, if we would allow Him to meet us there as on a new road to Emmaus. If his Spirit could make the letter that hid it vibrate with light and joy [in the Emmaus story], couldn't He who fulfills all the Scriptures also give full meaning to this one [i.e., the Qur'an] without altering anything on its face? However, it will be impossible to be convinced of this unless we approach the Qur'anic text with a poor and disarmed heart, ready to listen to any Word [*Parole*] that comes from the mouth of the Most High. Because, ultimately, how will we find the audacity and simplicity to climb the ladder together if we refuse from the start to believe that the same Spirit of God invites us to do so?

> Say: O people of the book! Come to a common word between us and you! (Q 3, 64)

3. An Ascending Path . . .

Beyond this parallel *lectio* that a contemplative living in an Islamic country may feel more directly called to undertake, I want to recall the many religious values of the Muslim tradition that have been an undeniable stimulus in my own fidelity to what I vowed by monastic profession. Between the pillars of Islam and the essential observances of all consecrated life there are obvious correspondences that make for successive rungs in a common ascension. The property of the rung, in fact, is to anchor deeply into each of the two uprights of the ladder on the same level if possible. It's a bit like a bridge that has been built from the opposing banks. It is when we attempt to define the *levels* of authentic spiritual progress that we are suddenly surprised to find ourselves so close.

We should enumerate some: the giving of oneself to the Absolute God, regular prayer, fasting, sharing of alms, conversion of heart, unceasing remembrance of the Presence that bears a Name (*dhikr*, ejaculatory prayer, the Jesus prayer), trust in Providence, the urgency of hospitality without boundaries, the calls to spiritual combat and to pilgrimage, which can also be interior. . . . In all this, how can we not recognize the Spirit of Holiness, of which no one knows from where it comes or where it goes (Jn 3:8), from where it descends or where it ascends? Its function is always to give birth from above (Jn 3:7), to draw onto an *ascending path* (*'aqaba*):

> How will you know what the ascending path is? It is freeing a slave, feeding at the time of famine an orphaned close relative or a destitute poor person. It is to be among those who believe, those who encourage each other to be patient, those who encourage each other to be lenient. Such are the companions of the right. (Q 90:12–18)

The list of *good works* to which we are called could be unceasingly multiplied by the heart's imagination (Saint Benedict lists seventy-three in chap. 4 of his *Rule*!). And they converge quite often, as long as we recognize the similar realities underlying potentially different expressions. Refusing to do so amounts to designing rungs with only one upright. It would be better just to take down the ladder!

A few concrete examples: Someone will undoubtedly ask whether our rung of *fasting*, which is kind of weak after all, really corresponds to that of the Muslim, who immediately thinks of Ramadan. I leave the answer to my friend Mohamed whom I asked what Ramadan meant for him. "It is," he told me, "a gift from God that draws us to Himself." And he added: "God's gifts are not always easy!" We think of the Cross . . . , of the Eucharist too. Why not put this [attitude] at the heart of fasting, which would turn it into *our daily bread*? The rung of *Jihâd*, so misunderstood by most Westerners, will regain all its evangelical resonance if we define it with Mohamed Talbi as "the effort to insert oneself into the perspective of God" [Talbi, *Un respect têtu*, 26]. It would be impossible for that *striving* to lead anyone into war against their fellow men; on the contrary, if we could manage it together, we'd all be disarmed.

This *ascending path* thus reveals itself as a "reciprocal conversion by which God commits us little by little (rung by rung), according to the degree of our faithfulness in the coming of his Kingdom" (Bishops of North Africa, 1979, 10/3) [*Chrétiens au Maghreb: Le Sens de nos rencontres*, Pastoral Letter of the Episcopal Conference of North Africa, May 4, 1979]. Among the happiest intuitions of our *Ribât* was our choice to live and deepen, during the six months between meetings, a theme belonging to both traditions and likely to keep us close on a daily basis: giving thanks, *dhikr*, covenant, the death of Jesus, conversion, fraternal love, unity, the spiritual life, the way of Mary, etc., and most recently, *called to humility*.

4. Called to Humility . . .

At the end of our last sharing, it seemed to us that any dialogue between believers of good faith must always begin there. Agreeing that God calls us to humility is logically to renounce claiming to be better or superior; it also tends toward a form of personal authenticity without which we could not dream of claiming the Truth.

Christians and Muslims know well that the path to conversion involves coming to greater integrity of life. How can we not admit the often-astonishing contrast between our human behavior and the faith we affirm? This tireless quest for a genuine interior and performative coherence will guide us much more surely in our encounter with the other, who shares this level of spiritual exigency with us.

You perhaps know that Saint Benedict, in his *Rule*, sets up a ladder of humility that can only be climbed by going down: "He who lowers himself rises!" The lowest rung is the fear of God. It is interesting that the root *RaHaBa*, which expresses *monk* in Arabic, technically connotes *fear*. Must one take that step? Why not? Isn't that where we open ourselves to being joined by the One who humbled himself by taking the lowest place on the ladder, a place no one will ever take from him? To unite with Him in this lowering is to begin to realize with Him the entire scale of degrees up to the last rung, namely, the love that banishes fear, which is also the one where the monk humbly honors his Greek root: *monos* . . . to be one with the Unique and a beloved turned toward the One.

Some say that humility is rare in the Qur'an. You have to know how to look for it. It characterizes above all an attitude before God that is necessary for any spiritual progress (Q 2:45; 3:199; 17:109; 21:19; 32:15); it is even a beatitude:

> Blessed are the believers who are humble in their prayers! (Q 23:1–2).

5. A Spiritual Emulation . . .

Let's go further. This open wound of a call to humility implies an attitude of mutuality that is easy to overlook. In his travels, John Paul II, addressing Muslims (in Mindanao, Nigeria, Morocco, and elsewhere), spoke of the need we feel for who they are, *for their love*. That new language is counterweighted by a long history of confrontations, so we will have "to change our old habits," as the Pope recognized in his Casablanca speech:

We must respect each other and also inspire each other to good works on the path of God. ["Address to Young Muslims," Casablanca, Morocco, August 19, 1985, *Documentation catholique*, 1985, loc. cit.].

The principle of spiritual emulation will not surprise Muslims; when we discuss it with them we evoke a well-known Qur'anic verse:

> If God had willed, he would have made you one community. But he wanted to try you by the gift he gave you. So vie with one another in good deeds. . . . (Q 5:48)

Here the faith of the other is an admittedly mysterious gift from God. Thus it calls for respect, as we will only realize its full meaning at the summit of the ladder, which leads us to God together. The gift made to the other is also intended to encourage me in relation to what I have to profess. To neglect [what we've been given] would be to fail to contemplate the work of the Spirit and our part in it.

However, must we not admit with Father [Youakim] Moubarac that spiritual emulation remains the *poor cousin* of Muslim–Christian dialogue? His testimony is better placed than anyone's to appreciate the spiritual treasure of humanity that has been created in everyday life between Christians and Muslims throughout the history of Lebanon. If the tragedy of that country cuts us right to the heart, it is because it directly threatens the spiritual conviviality that we cannot afford to forgo.

We should perhaps, very briefly, note the role of monks in the sacred history of this spiritual emulation. The bishops of the East who engaged in dialogue were monks, such as Theodore Abû-Qurra (eighth–ninth centuries) or the Patriarch Timothy I (780–823). Bishop Gregory Palamas (twelfth century), the theologian of hesychasm, was also a monk who engaged in many spiritual conversations with Muslim scholars. One of them told him: "The time will come when we will really listen to each other." "And I," said Gregory, "agreed and expressed the wish that this time would come quickly" [quoted by Olivier Clément in *Un respect têtu*, 263].

In the West, at least two Benedictines have left a lasting mark on this dialogue in a history that sorely lacks points of reference: the monk Hildebrand, who became Pope under the name of Gregory VII (see his 1076 correspondence with the Emir El-Nasîr of Béjaïa), and the Abbot of Cluny, Peter the Venerable, patron of the first translation of the Qur'an into Latin and contemporary of Saint Bernard. Of the latter, it is better not to speak here except to join and accept the serious reproach that the Secretariat for Non-Christians (as it was then called) addressed to the monks of the time through one of its spokesmen, Father John Shirieda, dated March 4, 1986, and as part of the preparation for Assisi:

> Christian monks of contemplative life do not always adequately live the reality of the Church. Often, they do not perceive the need to feel in communion with others, who are to be seen as images of God, brothers of Christ, and a dwelling place of the Holy Spirit.... The approach of different religions to a very deep level of spirituality is of paramount importance in dialogue. This is what the Holy Father reaffirms. It falls to the monks themselves to take the initiative in this type of dialogue, not on a purely intellectual level, but in lived experience. [*Bulletin of the Aide Inter-Monastères*, 1987]

The reproach, however, does not apply at least to one son of Saint Bernard whose message was able to cross so many borders even after he was cloistered: Thomas Merton, monk of Gethsemane. Of course, this *contribution of monks* is quite limited compared to the pure spiritual *ordeal*, up to the point of receiving the stigmata, experienced by the Poverello of Assisi.

6. The Allure of the Spirit!

Three testimonies, taken from everyday life, will help us understand that this emulation, when lived authentically, constitutes us as a people of God who are open and called to an extraordinary communion on the path of development.

(1) We had a *Ribât* encounter on the theme of fraternal love. We presented the Christian approach based on the parable of the Good Samaritan (Lk 10:25–37), and our Alawiyya friends developed the point of view of the Muslim tradition. One of the Christian participants saw fit immediately to underscore that fraternal love was specific to Christian faith. I can still see R., a *bon vivant* full of common sense, welcoming the remark with a quiet smile and then responding: "We just told each other, I believe, that God has called us, all of us, to fraternal love. No escape possible! We also said, it seemed to me, that we were all having a hard time following through. So let's not set out on the wrong path under the pretext that 'It's we who . . .' or 'It's us that. . . .' We are gathered in order to receive this call together and to help each other respond to it better. Perhaps experience has taught us some 'tips' that we can share in order to progress, all of us, along this not-so-easy path." That always seemed to me a beautiful illustration of what spiritual dialogue is in relation to theological dialogue. We acknowledge ourselves as being weak but growing, and we try to walk a part of the way together, supporting each other to go a little faster, a little farther, in the same direction opened by the Spirit.

(2) A few years ago, just before Christmas, N., whom we know well and who was then a student of [Islamic] canon law in Mecca, arrives with a grand Sudanese sheikh whom he introduced as a professor at his university and a Sufi. I propose a coffee; he declines. "I only came for one thing," he announces. "N. explained to me how you live, and I too belong to a *confraternity*. Thus I would like you to share with me the secret of your *path to God*. I will do the same by revealing to you the secret of my *tariqa*. You cannot refuse. God reveals His secrets to his Sufis only so they can share them with one another and help one another advance on His path."

Naturally, I was perplexed and speechless. What exactly was my *secret*? Playing for time, I asked him to start by explaining his to me... and while he was describing it— it was quite ritualistic—and commenting on it, ideas with some clarity came to me, new ones entirely!

(3) Ever since one day M. asked me, quite unexpectedly, to teach him how to pray, he got into the habit of coming to speak with me regularly. He's a neighbor. We have a long history of sharing. Often I would have to cut our time short or go whole weekends without meeting him when the guests became too numerous and absorbing. One day he found the right expression for setting me straight and arranging a meeting: "It's been a long time since we dug our well!" The image stuck. We use it whenever we feel the need to communicate in depth.

Once, teasingly, I asked him: "And at the bottom of our well, what will we find? Muslim water or Christian water?"

He looked at me, half laughing, half chagrined: "Come on, we have been walking together for so long, and still you are asking this question? You know that what we find at the bottom of the well is God's water!"

These three episodes from life, and many others, allow us to taste what another friend, B., a heating technician by trade and a Sufi by grace, would undoubtedly call *the allure of the Spirit*. In fact, I told him one day that I had started to study closely the Qur'anic texts referring to the Spirit of God. It seemed to me that they might reveal the key to the mystery that unites us beyond the differences over which we inevitably stumble. He replied to me: "We must not try too hard to figure out who the Spirit is. . . ." I knew he was inspired by a verse from the Qur'an:

> They ask you about the Spirit. Say: The Spirit proceeds from the command of my Lord. You have been given little knowledge. (Q 17:85)

But he added on his own: "Don't look too hard . . . it takes away its allure!"

> Each body tends, by virtue of its gravity, toward the place which is proper to it. . . . My own weight is my love: wherever I am carried, it is that which carries me. Your Spirit inflames us and carries us upwards: we burn, we ascend. We climb the ladder of the soul, and sing the song of degrees. It is your fire, your benevolent fire that consumes us, and we go, we ascend toward the peace of Jerusalem. What joy it was for me to hear this: "Let us go to the house of the Lord." It is our will, if it is good, which will make of this place our home, and we will have nothing more to wish for than to remain there forever. [Saint Augustine, *Confessions*, 13.10]

III. THE COMMUNION OF SAINTS IN LABOR PAINS

At its top, Jacob's ladder touched the heavens. The time has therefore come to give our ladder of Muslim–Christian dialogue, and the society it establishes, its point of support in the *beyond*. I have the feeling that a descending theology, which still imposes itself here and there, would have ensured the eschatological anchoring from the start. I note, however, that in the vision of Genesis, as in that announced by Jesus in Saint John, the angels begin by ascending . . . , and the logic of the Incarnation leaves us little choice. Here our ladder is firmly anchored in our common soil. Between the two uprights we have seen rungs that are more for climbing than for counting. And there, beyond the horizon, we are sure of finding our solid support in God, the stable Rock about which the Psalms sing. But we also find there His mystery, opaque to our eyes, impenetrable: *al-Samad*, one of His most beautiful names [Q 112:2]. So that the two uprights of our ladder can lean against Him, it is important that He be that and more than that. All of us, according to our respective faiths, must say what the emir 'Abd al-Qâdir wrote in a text affirmingly cited by Bishop Teissier:

> If you think and believe that God is what all the schools of Islam profess and believe, know that God is that and that he is other than that!
>
> If you think and believe what the various communities believe—Muslims, Christians, Jews, Zoroastrians, polytheists and others—know that God is that and that He is other than that. . . . None of his creatures worships Him in all His aspects. . . . [*Église en Islam* (Paris: Centurion, 1984), 33]

Our ladder, which was intended to be a path for society, nonetheless legitimately leans upon the reality of faith to which it is affixed: the assembly of the elect having made the passage from this world to the Father. There we contemplate the new Jerusalem in which "every man is born" (Ps 86:5) *through Christ, for Christ, and in Christ,* a Church that, far from withdrawing into itself, is *ecstatic,* according to the word of Paul VI on which Cardinal Duval was to give such a beautiful commentary in his pastoral letter for Lent 1980 entitled "Fraternal Presence."

1. A Mystery in Urgent Need of Being Incarnated

The mystery of universal spiritual solidarity has been felt throughout time, despite the implacable struggles that continue to occupy the forefront of our stage. A feeling prevails that the world would disintegrate of its own accord without the tireless intercession of those *apotropean saints* whom Massignon linked to the witness of Abraham. Whether there are seven or twelve, these *Abdâl* are like the poles of the universe. They stand alone on site and in place of everyone else, to raise their arms above the human fray, like Moses, preferably on the tops of mountains or in the hollows of valleys. Do we realize that Mount Lebanon is called Djabal el-Abdâl?

Some will say that popular belief in the Muslim world is often more restrictive than that, as was the case for a long time even among separated Christians. And it may be that the Qur'an itself inspires belief in the exclusion of non-Muslims from salvation, including the *People of the Book.* Indeed it is written:

> The worship of the one who seeks a religion outside of Islam is not accepted. This man will, in the hereafter, be among the losers. (Q 3:85)

However, the wider context speaks of those who neglect to seek God or who lose their way after having been believers. Remember that in an identical context Saint Cyprian of Carthage was able calmly to assert, "Outside the Church, there is no salvation," without anticipating the sectarianism doing so would engender. Let us therefore avoid reducing Islam to a rejection. Another verse expresses an openness that many of our friends practice with conviction:

> Those who believe, those who practice Judaism, those who are Christians or Sabeans, those who believe in God and the last day, those who do good; they are the ones who will find their reward with their Lord. They will then no longer feel any fear, nor will they be distressed. (Q 2:62)

Going further, and aligned exactly with my faith in Christ, I must recall here a Muslim friend whom I knew when I found myself confronted, along with my entire generation, by the harsh reality of what was called the *Algerian War*. He was a man of mature age, deeply religious and obviously upright; he taught me to speak about God with a more-than-human respect, and to approach Him with simplicity and trust. A deep affection was born. . . . This unlettered man did not hide behind words. One could feel that he was torn between his brothers and his friends, unwilling to betray one group for the sake of the other, thus putting at risk his own life and the responsibility for his ten children. He would express the gift [of fidelity] concretely, paying with his life for the protection of a friend, who was more at risk than he was during a skirmish with his brothers.

Since then, I have known that I can place at the destination of my hope, in the communion of all the elect with Christ, this beloved brother who lived the commandment of perfect love unto death. Like all the other mysteries of the Kingdom, it is up to us visibly to signify this *beyond* of the communion of saints, where Christians and Muslims and so many others share the same filial joy. How can we go about it other than by loving here and now, freely, those whom a mysterious design of God prepares and sanctifies through Islam and by living with them a Eucharistic sharing of daily life? Furthermore, it seems to me that, by accepting the urgency of incarnating this reality of a communion that is beyond us, we at least exorcize any hint of proselytism as well as the rigid idea that tends to reduce conversion to the passage from one religion to another. When in fact there is such a passage it is because, more than any human mediation, God has intervened, and that also commands respect.

2. Ora et labora!
Prayer and work: it has been said that these are the two lungs of Benedictine life; they are also those of *existential* dialogue as we have defined it. A true Christian presence in a Muslim environment must establish itself on both aspects of the faith. History shows that we are often tempted to favor one to the neglect of the other.

One thinks of the witness of Brother Charles [de Foucauld] and his religious family, so deeply linked to a permanence of work and contemplation among the poorest. Let us also remain faithful to the message lived by Bishop Tudtud of Marawi (Philippines), at the other end of the Muslim world:

> The Christian presence cannot be that of a reforming observer, donor, or benefactor. It is not a presence infused with an aura of superiority or experience. It is a presence of complete solidarity and genuine sympathy with Muslims on an equal level. All those who come to live among them must "take off their shoes" like Moses, because the land they are going

to tread is sacred: God is already present before they arrive. [See *Lien d'Oran*, March 1980, a publication of the Diocese of Oran.]

How do we live this at Notre Dame de l'Atlas in Tibhirine? We have fumbled along, becoming aware that we must be inventive on both fronts. After the country's independence, we moved from the classic arrangement of [employing] a certain number of salaried laborers to working the land that belongs to us alongside four or five partners. Since we're gardening, everyone has their own plot, and we share the harvests fifty-fifty. This requires conscientiousness and trust as well as solid agreement between us, even if only for how to share the water or the marketing. We can say that everything is going well!

When you are free from your occupations, get up to pray, and seek your Lord with fervor. (Q 94:7–8)

In the matter of prayer, we have allowed ourselves to be led. We began by accepting that Muslim guests who requested to do so could make a retreat among us in complete freedom, provided of course they respected what they came for, namely, an atmosphere of silence, solitude, and, if they wanted, participation in the work. With the Alawiyya, the group desired an encounter in prayer with our community as such. A long companionship with them has enabled us to invite friends and neighbors more widely to unite themselves to the encounters at Assisi in 1986 or Kyoto the following year. A further step was taken last year when we offered the locals a large hall that had become available to serve as a temporary mosque, while they awaited [the completion] of one planned nearby. Thus bell and muezzin either overlap or follow one another inside the same enclosure so that it is difficult not to welcome the call to prayer wherever it comes from, which is a reminder of the communion that prevails in the heart of Him to whom we turn with the same abandonment.

3. A Prostrated Community

> O you who believe! Bow down, prostrate yourself, worship your Lord, and do good. Perhaps you will be happy. (Q 22:77)

This simple verse invites us once again to signify our communion by responding together to a shared call for prostration.

First there is [the issue] of *praying with*. Many people wonder: "Is it acceptable? What common language would not be equivocal?" Some remain categorical [in their determination]: "Together while praying, if necessary; praying together, No!" No syncretism... even if the Holy Spirit reveals himself to be an expert in the matter (and without waiting for us to voice our agreement with the *Song of the Lamb*). One understands the cautious declarations that preceded Assisi; they were necessary *pro bono pacis*. Nevertheless, at the same time, in the intervention already cited, Father Shirieda said to the monks:

> It is important to live in solidarity, not only with those who suffer, but also with those who pray. Those who pray together, whatever their religion, are no longer strangers to each other, but true brothers who journey together toward God. Praying together is religious dialogue par excellence. [*Bulletin of the Aide Inter-Monastères*, 1987]

It was easy for us to accept [his advice]. In 1986, we'd already had a long experience of common prayer consisting of invocations, songs, listening, silence, sharing. A little story may help. The Assisi meeting was on a Monday. The day before, Sunday, the Church offered the Gospel of the Pharisee and the publican (Lk 18:9–14). Commenting on it, I noted that the pilgrims the next day, in Assisi, should join in the publican's prayer: "Have mercy on me, a sinner!" When around thirty of us met again on Monday evening, the Muslim friend who initiated the common prayer began exactly there: *"Rabbî, irhamnâ!"* Praying together, or together while praying? The question was irrelevant; we were a single community prostrated in the attitude of the publican.

"Do good!" [Q 2:195, etc.]. The Qur'an often expands on this invitation by listing what we call the *works of mercy*. [Muslims] provide alms or *zakât*. More profoundly, they urgently insist on treating one's neighbor as oneself, the Golden Rule for them and for us. A hadith specifies: "Men, all men, belong to the family of God, and among them, the most loved by God is the one who renders the most service to His family" (quoted by Talbi, *Un respect têtu*, p. 62). Together we must therefore learn to practice better and better that other prostration, which became quasi sacramental for us when Jesus, getting up from the table at the Last Supper, practiced it in the repeated gesture of washing the feet of every disciple, including Judas. "Do this in memory of me! . . . What I did for you, you must also do!" (Jn 13:1ff.).

Cardinal Duval never ceases to repeat that the Holy Spirit is at work in every gratuitous gesture of fraternal love . . . , perhaps even more reliably than in every prayer.

4. The Bond of Peace

Do not allow us to justify human disorders by invoking your Name. . . . O God, author of peace and justice, grant us true joy and authentic love, as well as lasting fraternity among peoples.

By leading the young people of Casablanca in this prayer, the form of which so closely follows that of their Muslim tradition, John Paul II was working for peace. He'd already designated peace as the sign and pledge of the service that believers alone can render to the world, provided they finally achieve mutual understanding. The great sign of Assisi 1986 is perhaps less the prayer itself than its intention—world peace—and the agreed-upon necessity of removing the boundaries and prejudices that keep the men of religion(s) from meeting shoulder to shoulder and smoking the peace pipe together.

The same Arabic root *SLM* establishes a relationship among three words that are not usually brought together: *Peace, SaLâM*, which is also one of the most beautiful names of God, a gift that the world cannot give itself; *iSLâM*, which is fundamentally *surrender to God* before being a particular religion, a disposition that is the source of interior peace and of the filial communion in Christ's *surrender of all to his Father*; finally, *ladder*, SuLLaM, like those of the great mystics, from Saint John Climacus to Ghazâlî, or Teresa of Ávila with her *castles* and *mansions*. Is not the ladder that we have tried to erect here ultimately in the service of peace, on earth as in heaven, among all men of *good will*?

Is this common vocation to offer the world a sign of mutual peace nothing but smoke and mirrors? Sticking to the facts, one could think so. It's a grace of our time to have it demanded of us: "What is the point of believing if we cannot say about all of you: 'See how they love one another!'?" How many young people today ask this question, particularly in the West, finding in it a pretext to seek God elsewhere!

Wars of religion(s)—including the Crusades—have always harmed the cause of God, and they will seem ever more intolerable. "You (together) are the salt of the earth; if the salt loses flavor, then what . . . ?" [see Mt. 5:13]. M. M., the usual spokesperson for the Alawiyya, wrote to me, sharing some ideas on our theme for these *Journées*:

> The North looks upon the South with contempt; the first, sick, the second, lost. . . . Thus a total imbalance, a failure. Today there remains only one hope among believers. . . . Humanity can forgive politicians or scientists, but it will never forgive believers, people who pray, for having abandoned it.

Clearly we still have much to learn if we're going to respect each other in a simple daily life of *living together*. Most mixed-religion households know something about this. Sometimes there's a rupture with all its trauma and displaced children, and without a lifeline. There are also some beautiful successes. I wish to pay homage to them as the first visible cells in that immense mystery of the communion of the beyond: "Where two or three are gathered in my Name, I am in their midst!" [Mt 18:20]. Regarding freely accepted celibacy for the sake of the Kingdom, it can be all the more a sign of God's love for the multitude, manifested in Christ, making available to the Muslims, among whom it is lived, a calm place in the heart of a man or woman, open in advance to the treasure that each person carries in secret.

5. An Unexpected Vocation

We are in effect witnesses to a mystery of openness, the direct heirs of the Roman centurion who came to believe while contemplating the open heart of Christ lifted from the ground. No more ghetto is possible, no more tomb, no other

Holy of Holies than that Heart. In Him, two are *one*, always, and everywhere.

An unexpected vocation? It is first of all about *difference*. We instinctively resist it, and yet it is everywhere, in creation and in ourselves. It is what specifies us as unique. It belongs to the mystery of God. The Holy Spirit testifies to this, uniting the Father and the Son via the Name by which each calls the other. Why can't the differences between Christians and Muslims, broadly speaking, have the sense of communion that is in God? John Paul II had, in this regard, very strong words: "If the order of unity is divine, then that of differences 'and divergences, even religious ones,' is therefore 'a human fact,' except of course 'those [differences] in which the genius and spiritual "riches" given by God to the nations are reflected'" (see *Ad gentes* 11) ["Address to the Roman Curia at the exchange of Christmas wishes," December 22, 1986]. This difference, say our Alawiyya friends, is the *mercy of God*.

Another unexpected vocation? Theology! Theology can be a bit presumptuous in occupying all the terrain of the Spirit, expertly managing what has always been said or done. Assisi was, in a way, the initiative of the Spirit seizing upon that of the Pope in favor of a shared, unpredictable, undeniable spiritual experience. No credible theology, henceforth, can ignore the perspectives opened by this *eloquent sign*. John Paul II recalls, as if to convince himself, with beautiful humility: "We are invited to reflect. What is its meaning? What is the key to reading it? Welcome 'this object lesson,' this 'catechesis intelligible to all . . .'" ["Address to the Roman Curia at the exchange of Christmas wishes," December 22, 1986].

Yet another unexpected vocation? That of he who is neither one nor the other, that is to say, neither Christian nor

Muslim. . . . In the Gospel, he has no other name than that of his given *community*: Samaritan, Canaanite, Roman . . . as if to escape the temptation of possessing him (her) by separating him from his family. Our God welcomes the Stranger into His house of prayer. It is up to us to be a sign of this divine hospitality in the names of this community *of origin, destiny,* and *insertion* which are inscribed on the three levels of our ladder. I think of Sheikh I. paying his respects at the grave of a Muslim without paying attention to that of a Jew on the other side of the wall. That night in a dream a voice tells him also to pray for the Jew. . . . But how can that be? He asks his father, who offers him the following verse as the only answer:

> The believers are brothers. Therefore establish peace among your brothers. Fear God! Perhaps you will be shown mercy. (Q 49:10)

So he goes back to pray at the other's grave. What will it take for Palestine to be a place of *peace among brothers* and not just a cemetery? Plant the sign of Assisi in Jerusalem!

6. *Lex orandi, lex credendi*

Tell me how you pray, and I will tell you what you believe. Our places of prayer have preserved at least one indication of the vocation to *gather,* which is linked to our respective faiths: synagogue, ecclesia, *djem'â* . . . : each has the same etymology. However, the outsider is often asked to remain at the threshold of the sanctuary that does not belong to his *tribe.* It was civil-secular society that invented multipurpose places of prayer in airports or large stores. Before that, history only recorded the changes of identity—church or mosque—following often deadly political fluctuations.

The prayer of the assembly itself has the vocation of illuminating the faith by deepening it, sometimes even by preceding it. Who can set the boundaries of the *we* that Jesus taught us to pray in the *Pater*? Note too that the Muslim *Fâtiha* expresses itself in terms of *we*. Michel Lelong did not hesitate to identify a parallel between these two foundational prayers.

Anyone who lives in a Muslim country feels the need to find in liturgical prayer the openness to the other that it is intended to signify, and most often he feels strongly supported by the very beautiful orations of the Vatican II missal. Sometimes, however, particularly in the *Liturgy of the Hours*, he stumbles over reductive expressions of his faith such as:

> May our prayer in the name of Jesus call forth your salvation upon all those who call on his Name. (Monday at None)

One day I asked Y., who was recently baptized, how he now felt about the *Adhân* (the call to prayer): disinterest? annoyance? refusal? He answered me simply: "I try to unite myself to Christ who offers this prayer to his Father. . . ."

Often we wish to pray for friends and deceased neighbors. Does it make sense to forbid officially mentioning them during the heart of the Eucharistic prayer? It would be so easy to adjust the formulation: Were not the unbaptized definitively "immersed in the death of Christ and already participants in his resurrection" [Rom 6:4] when they themselves tasted death?

Personally, I have often expressed the wish that the saints of the Old Testament whom Christ himself associated with the splendor of his Glory, whom the Qur'an mentions, whom Islam venerates, and to whom the Eastern Church has consecrated immemorial devotion be inscribed in the *propers* of our Churches; for the moment, Abraham has won his case. But Moses, Elijah, Melchizedek, Zechariah, and Elizabeth? Couldn't these great witnesses help us to enter, in our own way, into the most significant celebrations of the Muslim calendar? On this question, the little book by Fr. Michel Lafon is a starting point [*Prières et fêtes musulmanes: suggestions aux Chrétiens* (Paris: Cerf, 1982)].

Just as there is a *Council for Interreligious Dialogue* alongside the *Council for Christian Unity*, similarly, would it not be legitimate to introduce into the Roman Missal, following the *Mass for Christian Unity*, another mass for spiritual understanding and sharing among all believers? "May they all be one . . . !," says Jesus (Jn 17:21). Our internal divisions seem definitively to have distorted this prayer of Christ. If we could relearn it, as going beyond reconciliation simply among separated Churches, then surely we would be offered a better taste of the unity that exists among Christian brothers, an irremissible gift, which is perhaps veiled like holiness but similarly discernible. *I believe in the Church, one, holy.* . . . Perhaps Mary could help us to decipher this reality, if we would fully embrace the reciprocal hospitality lived in the mystery of the Visitation. The *mystery of faith* is the intercession of Christ, the unique firstborn of many brothers.

7. A Reciprocal Hospitality . . .

We profess, both of us, hospitality as a sacred obligation of our faith. He who generously shares his bread, his roof, his time with us, treats us like those *little ones* in whom Jesus, before him, recognized his brothers. And we in turn can decide to welcome him as Christ himself: "Come, blessed of my Father, into the Kingdom which has been prepared for you . . ." (Mt 25:31–35).

However, reciprocal hospitality logically should begin where Jesus sought all of us, in giving himself up *for the multitude, for the remission of sins*. It is paradoxically at the table of sinners that I learn best to embody, at whatever stage I find myself, the promised mystery of the communion of saints. The multiplied bread we have already been given to break together, Christians and Muslims, is that of absolute trust in the mercy of God alone. When we consent to join in the sharing, doubly brothers because we are *prodigal* and because we are *forgiven*, then something of the eternally ordained feast that gathers us in His House can be celebrated. Among us there is already a *table spread*, a mystery written but ever in need of understanding:

> Jesus, son of Mary, said: O God, our Lord! Send down unto us a table from Heaven spread [with food]! (Q 5:114)

This reciprocal hospitality is that of Mary and the beloved disciple at the foot of the Cross. Formerly, the Mother asked: "Who has borne me these?" [Isa 49:21] (Isa 49:18ff.). Today she asks simply: "How will this be done?" She was answered: "The Holy Spirit will take them under his shadow . . ." [Lk 1:35], and Mary lets herself be sheltered, ready to run to her cousin, welcoming and singing all the visitations of the Spirit from age to age. M. M., commenting from her Muslim perspective on the *way of Mary*, said to us: "The Holy Spirit is always with the ones who take Mary into their home!"

The mystery of the Visitation is indeed that of the most perfect reciprocal hospitality. It is good that increasingly the Church is placing it at the heart of the *haste* that carries her toward others. She is discovering her *Mission* as our brother, and Father Jean-Marie Raimbaud explained it last year at the opening of the Synod of his Church of Laghouat, so small and similar to ours in our desert:

> "Mission" under the action of the Holy Spirit is the confluence of two graces, one given to the sent, the other to the called, the non-Christian. The Christian strives to read what God is saying to him through the person of the non-Christian; he also strives, with his community, to be a visible sign, a Word as clear as possible of God, Father, Son, and Spirit.

Thus the *Magnificat* springs forth, infinitely taken up in the Eucharist.

Jean-Marie, who recently died, was more optimistic than I and spoke of confluence where I speak of parallel. But now he is telling us where the confluence lies, and we'll have to join him there, where God took him.

As we come to the completion of this too-long journey, I offer the words of a pastor who was suddenly torn from those whom he had guided by desert paths for more than twenty years. To him, along with many others, we repeatedly pose the question: "Watchman, how far gone is the night? Watchman, how far gone is the night?" And he has answered us, as the prophet (Isaiah) once did: "Morning comes, but also the night. If you want to ask the question again, come back!" (Isa 22:11ff.). Now that the fullness of the paschal dawn has risen for Jean-Marie, one Sunday morning, his life with God takes on the meaning of the message which concluded his *opening* of the Synod and which he communicated even in the way he lived his death:

> The Kingdom of God is there in your midst. Will we have poor hearts to welcome it?

We must return to the foot of the ladder planted in this night of men, and climb, rung by rung, the narrow path that transfigures the "companions of shadow into sons of light" [Jn 12:36]. Sometimes there's a lightning flash, "Light upon light!" (Q 24:35), the lamp-witness of a spiritual fecundity secretly preparing "the ultimate and radiant birth" [see Talbi, *Un respect têtu*, 42].

INTERMONASTIC DIALOGUE
AND ISLAM (1995)

"Intermonastic Dialogue and Islam" was delivered at the annual meeting of Monastic Interreligious Dialogue, an international organization of Christian monks and nuns and their functional equivalents in other religious traditions. De Chergé mentions two appendices in the article. In Appendix I, he provides the agreed-upon aims of the Ribât as-Salaam dialogue group. In Appendix II he compiles a list of relevant quotations, mainly from the Qur'an but also from the Bible and the writings of St. Bernard of Clairvaux. We did not translate the appendices, because they do not contain, exclusively, the words of Christian de Chergé. Al-Ghazâlî (1058–1111), of Persian descent, is among the most influential Muslim thinkers and writers in history, who, in part, sought to integrate Sufi wisdom with theological learning. The Iraqi mystic and writer Râbi'a al-Basri (716–801) is among the most important early Sufis and perhaps the best-known Sufi woman in history. While little is known about her biography, many stories describe her as having embraced a life of celibacy. The Turkish medieval thinker and poet Jalâl al-Dîn Rumi (1207–1273), with whose poem

---

"Dialogue intermonastique et Islam" was originally delivered as a talk at the annual meeting of Monastic Interreligious Dialogue in 1995, which met in Montserrat, Spain. It was published in *L'invincible espérance*, ed. Bruno Chenu (Montrouge, France: Bayard Éditions, 2010), 205–17.

de Chergé closes the article, is perhaps the best-known Sufi in history, certainly in the West. Louis Massignon (1883–1962) was a pioneering Catholic scholar of Islamic mysticism, who significantly influenced the modern Catholic Church's friendly turn toward Muslims and Islam.

Is there a place for an INTER-MONASTIC dialogue with Islam since, it is said, there is no "monasticism" in Islam? To ask the question is often to have answered it already. In fact, there is a kind of monastic disengagement in the interreligious dialogue directed toward Islam. More generally, is there room in an authentic monastic life for this type of gaze toward the other? Isn't it a distraction from contemplation?

The same question arises for the approach to all the other religious paths. It is Scripture and, even more so, Jesus himself, by his Spirit, who will say what should be learned from the Qur'an and from Muslim wisdom, in the name of welcoming the other, which is at the heart of the Gospel (and the *Rule* of Saint Benedict). Let us learn to practice this welcome without demanding reciprocity, in the name of the One who came to us freely!

A prerequisite therefore: to be in a position of WELCOMING and SHARING what is lived. *Implantation* in a non-Christian environment (Muslim, in this case) is not simply a *luxury*. It completely changes one's approach and creates a different sensibility. From our *place*, which is totally immersed in the Arab Muslim world, we would not have written in the same way the [Monastic Interreligious Dialogue] text entitled: "Contemplation and Interreligious Dialogue" (and it is regrettable that the document is the fruit of an exterior encounter only with Far Eastern "monasticism").

MONKS EXIST IN THE QUR'ANIC TRADITION

There are indeed four explicit mentions, not counting the very beautiful text of the sura of the Light (24) (see Appendix II): criticism of seeking honors and avarice (9:31 and 34); praise of modesty (5:82); the controversial verse: "They did not respect . . ." (57:27) with the hadith (= a saying attributed to the Prophet), contested, especially by Massignon: "No monasticism in Islam!" Additionally: "Our *sunna* (law) is marriage!," which shows that the monastic ideal is perceived in Islam to be directly linked to celibacy. Some spiritual Muslims have sought to experience it as purification in their quest for God, either provisionally (like Ghazâlî) or much more rarely as a definitive choice (e.g., Râbi'a).

THREE VITAL TIES WITH THE MONASTIC TRADITION

Obedience: it is at the heart of the Son, and therefore of the Gospel (and of the *Rule*). It is *islam*, since the very word means "surrender to God." The vows of the Benedictine tradition involving *conversion* of life and stability join a deep movement of the Muslim soul seeking to express, in concrete terms, its "surrender."

Ritual prayer (*opus Dei*): here, it is the whole people who are called to pray five times per day, and also to fast (month of Ramadan), and to give alms. These are the three *pillars* of the faith for *every* Muslim. A good number of Muslims think that monks are the only Christians who "pray," precisely because they have a regularity of office that mirrors their common path. "We do not see Christians praying," say our Muslim friends. This underlines the importance of a mutual presence in prayer.

Lectio divina: it is a primary and essential indication of "a God who speaks to men" [*Nostra Aetate* 3]. There is, on both sides, a REVELATION that has always had something to reveal about itself, which it is necessary to let speak, repeat, gloss, interpret, to write in calligraphy. . . . The spirituality of the *Night of Destiny* (around the 27th of Ramadan), where a verse can "descend" upon the believer as a word [*parole*] for him, is that of every true monastic *lectio*. It enters through the ear: "Listen!" "Read!" Together we are engaged in an adventure of *meaning*. In our way of reading Scripture, of reciting it, there is a path of sharing. A horizon offers itself to us: "Let us come to a common word!" (Q 3:64).

The spiritual dialogue is there: we do not know the true *meaning*; we do not truly live the Word [*Parole*]; we can help each other to be in accord with what God wants. This double humility serves as a prelude to mutual support toward improvement.

TWO CONSEQUENCES OF THE CONTENT OF THE DIALOGUE

At the level of moral values: in moral conduct, there are striking contrasts between us, especially if one sticks to a literal reading of a facile middle way, for Muslims, confronted by an evangelical ideal of holiness. As if all Christians live the ideal, while all Muslims are content with the minimum! In this regard, the monastic witness is helpful: it affirms the need for permanent struggle, *jihâd*; it acknowledges the fragility of our nature and its temptations; it finds support in communal emulation; it is linked to a concrete exercise of very daily virtues: regularity, work, justice, simplicity, mercy, etc.

At the level of the expression of faith: there too, there are some apparently insurmountable oppositions, many clichés, endlessly repeated as so many accusations against the *other*. There is a long history of ferocious polemics, where some monks have sometimes poured oil on the fire (see Saint Bernard) while others searched for "notes of agreement" (from Saint Gregory VII . . . up to Thomas Merton).

The purely theological dialogue is fruitless. The Holy Spirit can help to move beyond the dogmatic, for example, by inviting us to translate in terms of "common" faith the achievements of a spiritual sharing lived as an authentic encounter "in God."

SPECIAL TOUCHSTONES FOR AN INTERMONASTIC JOURNEY WITH ISLAM

The invocation of the *Name*: the NAME as a relation to God, and also in God: the ninety-nine most beautiful Names, and the Name of "Jesus," which is itself theophoric ("God saves"), the same for "Emmanuel" ("God with us"); *dhikr* and the Jesus prayer; the path of apophaticism: "He!" "You!"

The jealous *monotheism* of Jesus and his abandonment to the will of the Father, his prayer in faith, in the night.

The *way* of Jesus, gentle, humble, a feast for all, and the *sign* of Mary, with her "fast" (silence).

The *desire* for God, life as a "way" (*tariqa*), pilgrimage, quest, all a vocabulary of the road (including the *shari'a!*).

The gift of *prophecy*: a "charismatic" existence (apothegms and Sufis).

Surrender to God and the vocation to make good use of the earth: *ora et labora*.

Along these lines, one can read in Appendix I the concrete proposals that Christians and Muslims of the *Ribât* assigned themselves for defining the spiritual climate of a mutual approach engaging all of life.

CONCLUSION

It is indeed a question of "entering into the axis of the other," as Massignon desired. The other matters to me. It is as other, stranger, Muslim, that he is my BROTHER. His difference bears meaning for me, for who I am. It provides substance to our mutual relationship, as well as to our common quest for unity in God.

Encourage each other mutually. . . . When he calls you to Himself, together, God will explain to you the "why" of your differences, says the Quran (5:48). And the Gospel has Jesus saying: "The Holy Spirit will explain all things!" [Jn 14:26].

We must return to *hospitality* as a Benedictine constant, which has so many resonances in Muslim society in all its forms (again, the trajectory of Massignon):

- that of the *welcome* expected by the *Rule*: at the door, then at the guesthouse
- that of the *culture*: study of the language, customs
- that of *lectio*: there is a possible "monastic reading" of the spiritual tradition of the other, and above all of the Qur'an itself. Is it possible to respect the ways of God in the other if we don't try?
- that of the *liturgy*, of the *opus Dei*: gestures of prayer, common words or invocations, feasts to join, a shared silence as a Presence, honoring Friday, joining Ramadan

- that of *life*: so many things from everyday life made to serve as parables, as "sacraments" of encounter
- finally, that of *theology* . . .

Listen, if it is possible for you to listen:
To arrive at him is to leave oneself.
Silence, over there is the world of vision.
For them, the word is a GAZE. (Rumi)

MODERN SPIRITUAL MASTERS
Robert Ellsberg, Series Editor

This series introduces the essential writing and vision of some of the great spiritual teachers of our time. While many of these figures are rooted in long-established traditions of spirituality, others have charted new, untested paths. In each case, however, they have engaged in a spiritual journey shaped by the challenges and concerns of our age. Together with the saints and witnesses of previous centuries, these modern spiritual masters may serve as guides and companions to a new generation of seekers.

Already Published

Modern Spiritual Masters (edited by Robert Ellsberg)
Swami Abhishiktananda (edited by Shirley du Boulay)
Metropolitan Anthony of Sourozh (edited by Gillian Crow)
Eberhard Arnold (edited by Johann Christoph Arnold)
Pedro Arrupe (edited by Kevin F. Burke, S.J.)
Daniel Berrigan (edited by John Dear)
Thomas Berry (edited by Mary Evelyn Tucker and John Grim)
Dietrich Bonhoeffer (edited by Robert Coles)
Robert McAfee Brown (edited by Paul Crowley)
Dom Helder Camara (edited by Francis McDonagh)
Carlo Carretto (edited by Robert Ellsberg)
G. K. Chesterton (edited by William Griffin)
Joan Chittister (edited by Mary Lou Kownacki and Mary Hembrow Snyder)
Yves Congar (edited by Paul Lakeland)
The Dalai Lama (edited by Thomas A. Forsthoefel)
Dorothy Day (edited by Robert Ellsberg)
Alfred Delp, S.J. (introduction by Thomas Merton)
Catherine de Hueck Dogerty (edited by David Meconi, S.J.)
Virgilio Elizondo (edited by Timothy Matovina)
Jacques Ellul (edited by Jacob E. Van Vleet)
Ralph Waldo Emerson (edited by Jon M. Sweeney)
Matthew Fox (edited by Charles Burack)
Charles de Foucauld (edited by Robert Ellsberg)
Mohandas Gandhi (edited by John Dear)
Bede Griffiths (edited by Thomas Matus)
Romano Guardini (edited by Robert A. Krieg)
Gustavo Gutiérrez (edited by Daniel G. Groody)
Thich Nhat Hanh (edited by Robert Ellsberg)

Abraham Joshua Heschel (edited by Susannah Heschel)
Etty Hillesum (edited by Annemarie S. Kidder)
Caryll Houselander (edited by Wendy M. Wright)
Pope John XXIII (edited by Jean Maalouf)
Rufus Jones (edited by Kerry Walters)
Clarence Jordan (edited by Joyce Hollyday)
Walter Kasper (edited by Patricia C. Bellm and Robert A. Krieg)
John Main (edited by Laurence Freeman)
James Martin (edited by James T. Keane)
Anthony de Mello (edited by William Dych, S.J.)
Thomas Merton (edited by Christine M. Bochen)
John Muir (edited by Tim Flinders)
John Henry Newman (edited by John T. Ford, C.S.C.)
Henri Nouwen (edited by Robert A. Jonas)
Flannery O'Connor (edited by Robert Ellsberg)
Karl Rahner (edited by Philip Endean)
Walter Rauschenbusch (edited by Joseph J. Fahey)
Brother Roger of Taizé (edited by Marcello Fidanzio)
Richard Rohr (edited by Joelle Chase and Judy Traeger)
Ronald Rolheiser (edited by Alicia von Stamwitz)
Oscar Romero (by Marie Dennis, Rennie Golden, and Scott Wright)
Joyce Rupp (edited by Michael Leach)
Rabbi Zalman Schachter-Shalomi (edited by Or N. Rose and Netanel Miles-Yépez)
Albert Schweitzer (edited by James Brabazon)
Frank Sheed and Maisie Ward (edited by David Meconi)
Jon Sobrino (edited by Robert Lassalle-Klein)
Sadhu Sundar Singh (edited by Charles E. Moore)
Mother Maria Skobtsova (introduction by Jim Forest)
Dorothee Soelle (edited by Dianne L. Oliver)
Jon Sobrino (edited by Robert Lasalle-Klein)
Edith Stein (edited by John Sullivan, O.C.D.)
David Steindl-Rast (edited by Clare Hallward)
William Stringfellow (edited by Bill Wylie-Kellerman)
Pierre Teilhard de Chardin (edited by Ursula King)
Mother Teresa (edited by Jean Maalouf)
St. Thérèse of Lisieux (edited by Mary Frohlich)
Phyllis Tickle (edited by Jon M. Sweeney)
Henry David Thoreau (edited by Tim Flinders)
Howard Thurman (edited by Luther E. Smith)
Leo Tolstoy (edited by Charles E. Moore)
Evelyn Underhill (edited by Emilie Griffin)
Vincent Van Gogh (by Carol Berry)
Swami Vivekananda (edited by Victor M. Parachin)
Simone Weil (edited by Eric O. Springsted)